Aug. 1978

To Elder Merkley
It has been great to have
you on this mission. Bless
you always.

With Sincere Affection
Vaughn J. Featherstone

Do-It-Yourself
Destiny

Do-It-Yourself Destiny

Vaughn J. Featherstone

BOOKCRAFT, INC.
Salt Lake City, Utah

Library of Congress Catalog Card Number: 77-14716
ISBN 0-88494-329-1

2nd Printing, 1977

Lithographed in the United States of America
PUBLISHERS PRESS
Salt Lake City, Utah

Contents

Preface

Man is placed on earth to shape his life by his own decisions and exertions. Of all God's creations, man preeminently is here to act rather than to be acted upon. Whether our choices are made by decision or by default, each of us is molding an infinite future out of the material of a finite present. Destiny is a do-it-yourself project.

That concept and its implications, the essential message of this book, is usually more evident to age than to youth. Yet young people who are born to mature in the kingdom of God in this age need the head start which this clearer vision offers. This book, written particularly to young Latter-day Saints, offers a blueprint plus detailed guidance for their self-shaping project. It is the outgrowth of my experience both as a young person growing up and as an adult who has been privileged to work extensively with the youth of the Church over the years.

This book is in no way endorsed by the Church, and I assume full responsibility for its contents and for any error it might be found to contain.

While the book is written with young people in mind, the principles it expresses are equally important to persons of all ages. It is my hope that all who read it will feel uplifted, encouraged, and helped in their greatest project ever — the shaping of their destiny.

1

You're the Builder

Think back on what was the most memorable do-it-yourself project you have undertaken. Whatever your ability to work with your hands, you have undoubtedly done such a project at some time, whether it was a school assignment or a project you set for yourself at home.

The task may have been easy for you, moderately difficult, or rugged all the way, depending upon your aptitude and the nature of the task, but you felt impelled to do it anyway. And although you may have received suggestions and help from others, it was you who had to do the work and accept the responsibility for the finished product. In short, you were the builder.

You may not have thought of it in this way, but you're still a builder — every day, every hour, every minute. Whoever you are, that is a role you can't escape. You took on that part when you joyously accepted the Father's plan to send his children to a mortal earth, if not before that time. A verse by R. L. Sharpe expresses the role in this way.

> *Isn't it strange*
> *That princes and kings,*

And clowns that caper
In sawdust rings,
And common people
Like you and me
Are builders for eternity?

Each is given a bag of tools,
A shapeless mass,
A book of rules;
And each must make,
Ere life is flown,
A stumbling-block
Or a stepping-stone.

This verse may oversimplify the situation somewhat; for example, we all bring characteristics with us from our pre-existent state, so the "shapeless mass," the block of wood, we start with here is different for each one of us. But the general principle is clear and correct: each of us is the builder of his own soul and thus of his destiny. That means that you have on your hands the greatest do-it-yourself project of all time. It means too that although others may help with counsel and advice, even sometimes with a shove in the right direction, the person carrying ultimate responsibility for the finished product is you.

But is it really completely the individual's responsibility? you may ask. Doesn't the Lord take a hand in my life? Yes, he does — if you let him; if you make it possible. He will help you all the way. On the other hand, you can get plenty of help from Satan — if you make *that* possible. But neither of these beings will break his way into your life. The Lord won't and the devil can't. So unless you invite the devil in, the decisions are all yours. As the backwoods preacher put it, "The Lord votes for me and the devil votes against me; but I get to cast the deciding ballot."

I recall well some of my own attempts at do-it-yourself projects, and I would guess that my experience has not been so different from yours. In a woodwork project, for example, it was always difficult to get matching sides exactly alike; it was very easy to cut a little too deep; and, try as I might, some nicks and scratches insisted on appearing on the surface. On the other hand, there was a sense of pride in achievement when a part of the project turned out well, sometimes even perfectly, so far as the eye could detect. As I reflect on these experiences, I realize that it taught me an important principle: without exception, each stroke of the tool had its effect, good or bad. Each stroke either built toward the final product or detracted from that goal.

If you're like me you're not yet an expert on such projects. Nor are you perfect in this project of building you. But that makes no difference to the rules; for, as with the home or school project, every stroke takes its effect. There are of course simple, routine acts we do all the time which in and of themselves have no particular significance to the finished product — taking a drink of water, getting into bed at night, dressing in the morning, and so on. But with such obvious exceptions, virtually every thought, act and attitude, every conscious or unconscious decision to do or not to do something, either assists in the building or helps in the tearing-down process.

Let's suppose you want to be an athlete and you decide to build your body for that purpose. You draw up some rules for yourself — eating the right foods, getting to bed early, getting up early for a five-mile run each morning, and so on. Implementing such a routine requires a high degree of self-discipline, and self-discipline is never easy. Every time you keep a rule you have set, regardless of the temptations toward comfort, you have made a stroke that builds. Every time you rationalize your way out of keeping a rule, you have made a stroke in the opposite direction, one which will make it easier for you to do the same next time. Again, no stroke is without its effect.

The same applies to your other activities in mortal life. Life is dynamic, not static. Choices and decisions flood in upon you. You can't stand still; all the time you are either progressing or retrogressing, building or tearing down. Practice an instrument, learn a scripture, get an "A" in class, run a mile, and to that extent you're moving ahead. Give up your guitar lessons, leave the standard works unopened, let down in your school studies or your physical activity, and in those areas you're going backwards. There are only two directions in which to move, and only one person to make the decision — you.

The effect of some of these decisions on spiritual, eternal progress is immediately obvious. The use or non-use of the scriptures is an example. Consider too the Lord's words in the Doctrine and Covenants: "Seek ye out of the best books words of wisdom; seek learning, even by study and also by faith." (D&C 88:118.) The term "best books" used here of course includes the holy scriptures, but it was not meant to be confined to them exclusively. Reading any good book affects your life for the better — not merely during school days but for the rest of mortality and the eternities ahead. The Prophet Joseph Smith put it in this way:

"Whatever principle of intelligence we attain unto in this life, it will rise with us in the resurrection.

"And if a person gains more knowledge and intelligence in this life through his diligence and obedience than another, he will have so much the advantage in the world to come." (D&C 130:18-19.)

Then which decisions affect mortality only? Few if any of those we make each day. Notice the Lord's words about the relationship between "temporal" and spiritual things:

"Wherefore, verily I say unto you that all things unto me are spiritual, and not at any time have I given unto you a law which was temporal; neither any man, nor the children of men; neither Adam, your father, whom I created.

"Behold, I gave unto him that he should be an agent unto himself; and I gave unto him commandment, but no temporal commandment gave I unto him, for my commandments are spiritual. . . ." (D&C 29:34-35.)

Here the Lord says that to him all things are spiritual and that he has never given us a law that was temporal. The dictionary defines *temporal* as "of or relating to time as opposed to eternity; of or relating to earthly life." Now, if the Lord has never given a temporal law, one which related only to mortality, if to him everything is spiritual, it would be smart for us to take the same attitude and approach. Then we would not try to separate what we call spiritual from what we call temporal or mortal; and we would realize clearly that every choice we make between something good and something less good or better has a bearing on our spiritual development and thus on our eternal destiny.

Let's take a look at some of the laws God has given men. The Word of Wisdom might seem to be for the body only, for mortal life. Not so. A healthy body promotes spiritual health, activity in the Lord's service, and hence a growth that has immense significance not only here but in the eternities to come. On the other hand, from my observation it seems to me that it would be pretty difficult to concentrate on spiritual growth if racked by a smoker's cough or enslaved by liquor.

The law of tithing comes out in similar terms. The money it involves, the tenth we contribute, is of the earth; but, like everything else on earth, it is spiritual to the Lord. That is, it is intended for our spiritual growth. We grow if we use it wisely, unselfishly. Tithing is one way we show unselfishness, a desire to sacrifice for the Lord's cause.

If you examine all the other commandments of God, all given for our benefit, you will reach a similar conclusion. The end result of each law is spiritual, growth-producing for those who follow it. This was true even of the temporary Mosaic law, with its detailed, specific, apparently restrictive provisions. It was a schoolmaster, Paul said, to bring the people to Christ the Savior. Without such a law the Israelites, the Lord's chosen people, would have become like the heathen nations around them.

As it was, they too frequently and too willingly succumbed to those surroundings, and this eventually led to their downfall. There are those today who similarly surrender to their surroundings, frequently with a sense of giving up not only the fight but the responsibility. They want to put the building responsibility on others, even on impersonal forces. "My parents were divorced, and I didn't have a proper home life," one will say. Another will blame his social environment; "I grew up in a rough neighborhood, with no LDS friends, and I got in with the wrong crowd."

Too often, those who blame their situation on outside forces are something like the boa constrictor in the story. Foraging for food, the snake spied a rabbit and promptly devoured it. A little later he writhed his way into a small space between two fallen logs. It was a squeeze to get his head through but he managed reasonably well thereafter until the bulge about a third of the way down prevented further progress. He started to back out, when just ahead of him sauntered another unsuspecting rabbit. The temptation was too great, and soon the second rabbit had followed the first. Now the snake could neither advance nor retreat, and when a man came down the trail a few minutes later the snake was quickly despatched.

Now, the snake might have felt that he was the victim of circumstances. If he was, he made them by his overpowering taste for rabbits. Many a person, having acquired bulges in his character that hold him back from paths that the bulgeless ones frequent, similarly ascribes the blame to "circumstances" rather than to his addiction to rabbits. All of which brings to mind Elder Sterling W. Sill's story of the sales manager who asked the salesman how his sales were going and received the reply, "I'm doing as well as can be expected, under the circumstances." "What on earth are you doing down there?" was the manager's response.

"Experience," someone wrote, "is not what happens to a man. It is what a man *does* with what happens to him." Under such a definition, we change circumstances into experience by acting upon them. God created "both things to act and things to be acted upon," said Lehi. Circumstances may or may not be God-given, but they certainly are to be acted upon. As a child of God, you are one who is created to act and not to be acted upon.

Circumstances, then — environment, handicaps, apparent misfortunes — may influence us but must not be allowed to govern us. There are too many examples of unpromising beginnings which brought forth great characters for us to accept such a concept of inevitability. No, no one can opt out of the role of do-it-yourselfer — now or ever.

In that case, the smart thing is to do the best possible job on this project of building your destiny. After all, you can't live just on food and drink and sleep. That would be an animal-type existence. A true child of God, like his divine Parent, lives on meaning and purpose. So first you have to be clear what it is you are building.

A traditionally absent-minded professor was distressed when he couldn't find his ticket to show the train conductor. "That's all right," said the conductor, having witnessed two or three minutes of fruitless search. "I'll go through the train and then come back to you. I expect you'll find your ticket by then."

"That's all right from your point of view," responded the

professor, "but it doesn't solve my problem. Unless I find my ticket, I won't know where I am going."

You don't have to be like that professor. You know where you're going, what you're building for. In gospel principles you have the best kind of general rules for building. And your patriarchal blessing, plus the results of inspiration and personal guidance you can obtain through prayer, will give you a developing blueprint.

With the building rules clear and the blueprint established, perhaps the next order of priority is your attitude toward the quality of the workmanship. Remember, you are not building merely to please the outward eye. Your project is not like building a cabinet, for instance, the back of which goes against the wall and therefore usually takes inferior material and finish. For your building project nothing less than best-quality work throughout will do.

Phidias, the ancient Greek sculptor, had the right idea on this. Sculpting an heroic-sized figure of a goddess, he spent hour after hour carving the hair on top of the head. When a young man asked him why he spent so much time and care on this intricate detail which was too high up for anyone to see, the reply was immediate and forthright. "My boy," he thundered, "man may not see my workmanship, but the gods will."

There's one big difference between the standard do-it-yourself project and the job you have in building a better you. You can patch here and there in your home projects, but a serious mistake may mean scrapping the material and beginning again. As against this, your major life's project has a decided advantage: virtually no mistake is irreversible. With the tool of repentance you can correct every error and put the material in condition again for the building process to continue.

As for the building tools themselves, many of the most important ones are discussed in the following chapters. You won't necessarily be able to use every one of them perfectly at first. Skill in the use of any tool requires practice. The important thing at this stage is that you recognize your role as the builder of you, be aware of the building tools, and resolve to use them with increasing skill throughout life.

But don't fudge on the building rules, don't skimp on the

materials, and don't use inferior tools. If you do, you may find yourself in the position of the builder who constructed the house for the wealthy man's friend.

The rich man approached the builder. "I want you to build me the best house you possibly can. It is for a friend of mine of whom I think highly, so be sure you put into it all your skill and creativeness. I want you to spare no expense to produce the finest home for my friend. Use only the best materials and workmanship. Structure it solidly, finish it elegantly, and furnish it beautifully, so that I can present it to my friend with pride and confidence. I leave the details all to you. I will return when the house is complete."

The builder agreed to proceed as instructed and commenced the task. The plans were drawn, the blueprints took shape, and construction began. As the work progressed, the builder began to see ways to save himself time and to make some money. No one was going to inspect the construction work, and the finish would hide it all anyway. He began to cut corners — used poor materials he obtained cheaply, ignored some of the electrical and plumbing rules designed for safety and permanence, and bought furnishings that looked good but would fade and deteriorate in a few years. He congratulated himself that by charging for the best workmanship and materials he would make a lot of money on this project.

When the house was completed it looked the part — new, elegant, a home anyone might desire. Only the builder knew its defects, and these probably would not show up for a few years anyway. When the rich man returned, he and the builder went together to see the new house.

"My friend," said the rich man, as together they surveyed the scene, "this certainly is a fine-looking home. Now I have a surprise for you. I told you I wanted it built to give to a friend of mine. You are that friend. It has been built by you and for you, and I now give it to you. It is yours. Live in it forever and enjoy it."

Those last words could apply to your building project. Certainly you will live in it forever. Will you enjoy it? That depends on you, the builder.

2

The King's Son

Now that you recognize yourself as a builder, what kind of block do you personally have to build with? Let me quote you a poem with a message.

This I beheld, or dreamed it in a dream: —
There spread a cloud of dust along a plain;
And underneath the cloud, or in it, raged
A furious battle, and men yelled, and swords
Shocked upon swords and shields. A prince's banner
Wavered, then staggered backward, hemmed by foes.

A craven hung along the battle's edge,
And thought, "Had I a sword of keener steel —
That blue blade that the king's son bears — but this
Blunt thing!" — he snapped and flung it from his hand,
And lowering crept away and left the field.

Then came the king's son, wounded, sore bestead,
And weaponless, and saw the broken sword,
Hilt-buried in the dry and trodden sand,

And ran and snatched it, and with battle-shout
Lifted afresh he hewed his enemy down,
And saved a great cause that heroic day.

                                      — *Edward Rowland Sill*

Actually this poem has more than one message for you. The author gave it the title "Opportunity," and in that sense the poem conveys the concept that the opportunity is always there even if it must be snatched from apparent failure. But at the moment our concern with this poem is its implications for a king's son or daughter. For that is just what you are — a king's son or daughter. And it goes without saying that, just as in the poem, higher standards of excellence are expected of a prince or a princess.

Monarch's ancestry usually is hard to come by. Genealogy researchers in many countries have spent thousands upon thousands of dollars seeking to demonstrate their descent from a royal line. Perhaps an ancestor has dropped a hint in some document indicating a descent from, say, William the Conquerer or some other king. This is enough to set any genealogist's heart aflutter, and for the more susceptible the search can become intense.

The trick then is to tie in with a line which has already established its lineage back to that king. There are many advantages if this lineage can be established, and especially for the LDS genealogist, because usually the lineage of a king has been worked out for many previous centuries, frequently back to the pre-Christian era and sometimes even beyond that. And it has even been suggested, no doubt by some of us whose earthly lineage does not aspire to those heights, that the prestige value of tying into such a line has been known to influence the genealogist not to inquire too closely into the evidence.

The basis for earthly lines of royalty in the past were notoriously precarious. Sometimes conquest on the battlefield simultaneously set up one royal line and extinguished another, so that royal descent thereafter had hung in the hazards of one battle. Court intrigue, execution, and even assassination took their toll, cutting off one royal line and founding another. But your royal lineage is on a much firmer basis. There is never any call for you to fudge on the records in order to establish your royal descent. It is inescapable. You couldn't get away from it even if you tried. You have a three-way claim to royal descent, two of them historic and secure, the third an ever-present opportunity.

About four thousand years ago a great man was told by the Lord, "as many as receive this Gospel shall be called after thy name, and shall be accounted thy seed, and shall rise up and bless thee, as their father." (Abraham 2:10.) You are a descendant of this great man, who was named Abraham. He was noble in the best sense of that term, far superior to those who claim noble lineage in the merely worldly sense.

Yet Abraham was not a recluse or a hermit, a man who lived his life out in meditation far from normal earthly pursuits. He was an ancestor to be proud of in every way, a man of action, a leader who met problems head-on and found practical solutions for them. When several kings attacked nearby cities and carried away spoil and captives, including Abraham's nephew, Abraham quickly organized a small military force from his own band, pursued and routed the enemy, and carried back the goods and captives they had taken. Throughout the land among the heathen nations he was acknowledged for his greatness and power. "Thou art a mighty prince among us," said the Hittites to him on one occasion. (Genesis 23:6.)

A mighty prince indeed was our ancestor Abraham. So was his grandson Jacob, from whom you are also a descendant, another man of physical strength and vigor. "Thy name shall be called no more Jacob," the Lord told him, after he had successfully met a powerful challenger in physical combat, "but Israel: for as a prince hast thou power with God and with men, and hast prevailed." (Genesis 32:28.) We could go on to talk about Ephraim, Jacob's birthright grandson, whose descendants provided the kings for the kingdom of Israel after its split with the kingdom of Judah, and from whom most likely your patriarchal blessing indicates your descent. The point has been established, however. We might just add that, as modern revelation tells us, Abraham and Jacob have already received the reward of their noble lives on earth and are gods.

Yet significant as this great earthly lineage is, your other historical claim to a kingly lineage by far predates it and outshines it. Quite literally, you are the son or daughter of God our

Heavenly Father, the Organizer and God of the vast universe around us. With the same literalness and reality with which your earthly father is the father of your physical body, our Heavenly Father is the father of your spirit body. You readily recognize characteristics inherited from your earthly parents. A moment's thought will tell you that you have also inherited characteristics from your divine Father. The superimposed physical body may be either stifling or releasing those inherited splendors, depending upon your responses to the Spirit's influence, but they are there. It could not be otherwise, for you are an offspring of the Great King.

While past history presents you with a noble and kingly lineage for both your physical and your spirit bodies, there is yet a third level of princely living, a level which combines both the physical and the spirit bodies. This one however is not automatic. This one is a matter of choice for you. Only you can make it history.

The apostles Paul and John refer to Jesus Christ as the King of kings and Lord of lords. Wouldn't it give you a special relationship to him, and therefore a special degree of royal descent, if you could somehow be adopted as his son or daughter? Well, you can. How? By being born again, by experiencing the rebirth of the Spirit.

Jesus taught this principle to Nicodemus during his earthly ministry. Two thousand years before that, when Father Adam had received his rebirth through baptism by water and with fire and with the Holy Ghost, the Lord told him "and thus may all become my sons." (Moses 6:68.) King Benjamin saw the effect of the change which had come upon his hearers as they listened to his impressive sermon. "And now," he said, "because of the covenant which ye have made ye shall be called the children of Christ, his sons, and his daughters; for behold, this day he hath spiritually begotten you; for ye say that your hearts are changed through faith on his name; therefore, ye are born of him and have become his sons and his daughters." (Mosiah 5:7.)

If you want to know how you can be born of Christ in this way, perhaps the best scriptural summary in single-verse form is another passage in King Benjamin's address — Mosiah 3:19.

With such a striking ancestry and a future of such limitless promise, how should you and I behave? Shouldn't the knowl-

edge of these matters lift us above the common run? Shouldn't it
fire our souls with an inflexible resolve to cultivate the virtues
and qualities that go with true nobility of character — courage,
honor, faith, diligence, dependability, compassion, and those
other characteristics that make up just an all-round goodness? In
short, shouldn't it inspire us to want to obey the King's commands?

When we think of the rule of kings our minds tend to fly back
to medieval times, to the days when "knights were bold," to the
age of "romance and chivalry." I fancy, however, that to have
been a commoner in those days was a little less than thrilling or
romantic, since laws were harsh, monarchs were absolute in
their rule, and the king's whim or will prevailed. There wasn't
much fun in obeying the king in those days.

As an institution, the earthly king was not the Lord's idea.
When the Israelites clamored for a king, the prophet Samuel first
rehearsed to them the Lord's warning: a king would take their
sons for the army, their sons and daughters for his servants,
their animals for his work, their property as taxes to support him
and his palace economy. The typical king was selfish and arbitrary and obsessed with the idea of his own power. He largely
defined the laws, published them to the people through his
ministers and servants, and required that his subjects, including
his own family, conform to his will. They might not always do
this willingly, but do it they would.

Our divine King of course operates on an entirely different
basis. In giving us laws, as in all else, he is completely unselfish.
Just as he did when he lived on earth, he works for us and not for
himself. The commands of this King, unlike the absolute kings
of the past, are designed to make us free. "Ye shall know the
truth," he said, "and the truth shall make you free." (John 8:32.)
This of course is the only freedom really worth having — freedom from ignorance and sin, a freedom which only comes as we
learn and abide by his benevolent laws.

This makes the King we give allegiance to entirely different
from all earthly kings. In his life on earth he was not pampered
by luxurious living and in fact had absolutely no privileges
above those of the common people. He learned obedience, we
are told, by things which he suffered. He knows how rough the
road of life can be, and therefore he is sympathetic to our

stumblings along it. Even more, as he reminded us, he descended below all. There is a proverb which says, "He who pays the piper calls the tune." Our Savior has certainly "paid the piper." But for all that, he never calls the tune in an arbitrary way. This makes it all the easier to obey him. In our preexistent life we were well aware of his assignment as our Savior and King. With what eagerness we then assented to our own assignments on earth! With what willingness we agreed to do the King's bidding here!

As we contemplate the high standards of behavior expected of us as sons and daughters of the King, we find few earthly examples to emulate. For the most part, the term *nobility* has been used to imply a superiority based on birth and a determination on the part of those who possessed it to maintain it. It has meant resenting any slight and avenging every insult, real or imagined. But there have been notable exceptions in which the prince has shown a true nobility of character. Jonathan was such an example.

Jonathan was the son of Saul, first king of Israel. His friendship with David was of classic proportions, a pure and deep love which only the closest of friends can know. As Saul's character and mental balance deteriorated and his jealousy increased in the face of David's deserved popularity, he sought to murder David. Bitterly he remonstrated with Jonathan on the young men's friendship. Did not Jonathan understand that all the time David lived, the kingdom could never come to Jonathan? Jonathan was unconcerned about this factor. If the Lord wanted David to be king, that was all right with him, for he saw in David a soul as noble as his own. Against Saul's threats Jonathan helped to save the life of the man who would become king in his place. He himself died on the same battlefield as his father, courageously defending a lost cause.

Consider too the character and conduct of four other princes, the sons of King Mosiah. Formerly rebellious against both the earthly king and the heavenly King, after their repentance they were so heavily involved in carrying out their King's commandments that "they were desirous that salvation should be declared to every creature, for they could not bear that any human soul should perish." Armed with this conviction and a powerful faith in God, they marched boldly into the heart of

Lamanite territory, risking their lives to bring the heavenly King's commandments to a hostile and murderous people. Putting aside all thoughts of self in a way to merit the approval of the great King, they served that people for fourteen years and by their conduct and teachings were the means of bringing many thousands of them to the truth of the gospel. These men certainly knew how to behave as the sons of the king. They typify for us the difference between earthly and heavenly yearnings, between the typical arrogance of the seats of the mighty and the service of those who, as Jesus explained, become chief of all by being servants of all.

I remember hearing a Church speaker tell of an experience he had in a gathering he was obliged to attend in which there turned out to be a considerable amount of drinking and revelry. He observed that one man in particular as well as himself kept aloof from the proceedings. He engaged this man in conversation and eventually came around to asking why this man had not joined in with the others. The reply he received was : "Oh, it wouldn't be right for me to do that. I am a member of a royal family."

You too are a member of a royal family. You too must not stoop to ignoble acts, must not betray your heritage, even though you are exposed to wickedness, to vile and perverted things which servants of Satan are pushing upon the world in this generation. Have no part in all this. Shun it. Remember that you are, as Peter put it, "a chosen generation, a royal priesthood, . . . a peculiar people." (1 Peter 2:9.) Tread the royal road as your King has before you.

Like the kings of old, that King sends you his word through his ministers — in our case, the scriptures and the living prophets. Though the message itself will always be clear, there may be times when you will not fully grasp why his word to you is to do this or not to do that. But a king is there to be obeyed; and while you may not fully understand a commandment at this point in time, you do understand that your king has your interest at heart and that keeping that and every commandment will ultimately prove to have been for your good.

Naturally, a prince or princess expects an inheritance from the king. If you behave like the royalty you are, that inheritance will surely be yours. The King who has infinitely more to offer than any earthly monarch has promised you "all that my Father hath," in those circumstances. You even have a crown awaiting you, for he plans to make you no less than a king or a queen.

As you strive for that crown, remember that the pattern is the life of the King himself, our Elder Brother, the Son of the Great King. That life was a flawless reflection of the noble birthright which he and each of us has. Totally loyal and dedicated, he never deviated from the kingly route. And this unwavering course earned him the Great King's commendation: "This is my Beloved Son, in whom I am well pleased."

A similar commendation can be yours one day. You have the pattern and your own block of wood. Build well, prince or princess. In the words of President Harold B. Lee, "Be loyal to the royal in you."

3

Who's at
the Controls?

Physically speaking, for most of you who read this book "the living is easy." Modern inventions and technology have produced living conditions which would have been the envy of kings in former eras. In the U.S.A. in particular, which has one of the highest standards of material living in the world, we live in comfortable, centrally heated (and frequently air-conditioned), beautifully furnished homes where a turn of a tap delivers hot water to two or three elegant bathrooms and a touch of a switch brings power to drive our innumerable appliances, tools and gadgets. Two or three sleek cars stand ready to transport family members anywhere at any time. Meanwhile the advertising media constantly assail our eyes and ears with new inventions and refinements designed to bring us more of the same thing — easy living.

Now, no one in his right mind is going to object to modern conveniences or want to step back into the "good old days" of the horse and buggy. Physical comfort is an inevitable mark of an advanced standard of living. But it should be kept in its place. Comfort, pleasure and ease are not the end of existence, and to pursue them as if they were is to go contrary to life's true purpose.

That purpose is growth, and growth never comes by sitting around and taking life easy. Part of growth is difficulty, even hardship, for as one writer expressed it, "a kite rises against, not with, the wind." "It must needs be, that there is an opposition in all things," said Lehi, the Book of Mormon prophet. (2 Nephi 2:11.) So although we don't necessarily have to go out and seek discomfort and hardship, we are to expect it as a natural part of life rather than suppose continuous ease and luxury to be our right.

Why do I make so much point of this? Because of the bearing it has on the vital principle of self-mastery. Self-indulgence wears down the will until slothfulness and appetite take control. This is the direct opposite of the gospel way, under which the appetites and passions are to be kept under proper control as a necessary part of the continued reach for perfection. Thus self-mastery is at the heart of gospel living.

The story is told of an ancient Greek philosopher being approached by a mother bearing a newborn child. "What is the most important thing I can teach my child?" she asked. "Teach him to deny himself," was the sage's reply.

Why would he say that? Because the ability to control one's words and deeds by an act of will constitutes the mastery of self and has been recognized throughout the ages as a mark of greatness. That ability only comes by a pattern of life which deliberately chooses more difficult tasks over easier ones.

As this pattern is pursued, the difficult becomes easy, the impossible merely a peak which looms just beyond the difficult and invites our attack. Accomplishment multiplies as mind and body and spirit, welded into an unbeatable team, stride forth to conquer.

The being who was the Master in every way was the complete master of self. The trial and crucifixion of Jesus Christ portray a person whose superb control remained undisturbed in the face of fatigue, hunger, ridicule, indignity, and finally physical agony. In contemplating this great example we glimpse the meaning of the line, "Master yourself, and enemies hammer at the gates in vain."

The self-discipline that leads to self-mastery is necessary in all areas of our lives, including the physical; for as we saw in chapter 1, all true growth is spiritual in its impact. The disciplines can and should begin at an early age. Frequently they are sparked by the motivation of athletics. This happened to me when I was about eleven, at which time circumstances combined to produce a very important development in my life.

My older brother, Steve, approximately 2½ years older than I, had some very strong interests. At the age of fourteen he weighed about 175 pounds and was over six feet tall. He started lifting weights and doing chin-ups; he bought weight-lifting magazines and began to develop his body; he organized a schedule for developing physical fitness and followed it faithfully. I remember to this day the different weight-lifting exercises used to develop different muscles. Steve could do over fifty push-ups, touching his chest on the floor each time. He was the push-up champion at his junior high school.

I watched Steve with great interest and then started doing the things he did. It was about this time that one of the five brothers in our family became ill with scarlet fever, and as a result we were all quarantined for four weeks. That meant we couldn't even go to school. The day we were to be released from quarantine, the doctor came down to check us out and discovered that one of the younger brothers was just coming down with scarlet fever — so we were quarantined for a further three weeks. I would like to share with you what happened during that seven-week period.

With Steve leading out, each day we would have athletic contests and conditioning exercises. We would put the shot, do the high jump, do push-ups and chin-ups, run around the yard (we couldn't leave the yard), and do all kinds of physical exercises. We did this every day routinely. Before the seven weeks were over I could do sixteen or more chin-ups and seventy-four push-ups, and every physical ability had increased proportionately.

We even had contests at doing the dishes. Steve would have me clear off the table and get everything ready, then we would time ourselves doing the dishes. I think we hold the world's record for speed and quality dishwashing and drying.

Sometimes Steve and I would have disagreements in which we would do battle. Looking back, I suppose I was an obnoxious little kid; at any rate, Steve would "clean my plow" regularly. This happened quite often. I remember that one day my uncle told me of two brothers who fought each other as we did. He said that at one time the younger brother decided he had been beaten up once too often by his older brother. He thought about it and made an iron resolve to give that brother a beating such as he had never experienced before. With this resolve, and inspired with fire for the deed, he found his older brother, tore into him, and really gave him a beating.

I was impressed with the story. I thought, "That is what Steve deserves; I have been beaten up for the last time." I made an iron resolve and inspired myself also with fire for the deed, then I sought out my older brother. When I found him I said: "I've been waiting for this for a long time. You'll be sorry you ever touched me when I'm through with you today." Then I tore into him with a wild fury. I believe that was the worst beating I ever took.

I'm sure my mother wondered whether any of her five sons would grow to manhood. I think she expected us to be crippled or maimed for life.

My brother Steve had a most powerful impact on my life. He had great strength and was a model of a man after whom I could pattern my life. During our growing-up days at home he was the object of my hero worship. When he played football in high school I would polish his shoes. I would wash his shoelaces in Clorox; then I would iron them. No one had better-looking shoes and laces than my brother. He played full back on the football team. I too wanted to play fullback. He ran the half-mile, so I ran the half-mile. As a result of this emulation, in my youth I was in excellent physical condition.

When I went out for sophomore football in high school, Steve trained me. I would put on my football uniform and we would go out in the backyard and square off. We would practice my defense by his carrying a ball right over the top of me. Then I would carry the ball and he would tackle. We really had some bruising sessions. He taught me physical discipline, mastery over my physical body. He taught me to suffer and hurt in silence. I could never let him know how much he hurt me; I had far too much pride for that. That kind of training made me fearlessly aggressive on the football field against others of my own age.

As I look back on my life I recognize that I was disciplining myself to accomplish strenuous feats on the physical plane. But that plane is not enough. To develop true self-mastery we must apply the same rigorous discipline and high standards in the mental and spiritual areas.

The word *self-mastery* suggests complete self-control, unquestioned direction by the master over the servants. With the master in command, our acts and thoughts are under total control. All of us know men and women like this, people who seem to be completely self-controlled. Their actions are directed by their will and not by random emotions. Furthermore, they make their own decisions regardless of the attitudes of the crowd.

This important element of self-mastery, the ability to withstand the pressures of the crowd, was brought to my mind by an impressive experience I heard of some years back when I was working with the Explorers. That summer we took our Explorers down the Snake River in canoes. Each night on this trip we had a campfire, and around the fire one of the men gave a spiritual thought. One of the men whose turn was coming up said to me, "I don't think I have anything to say." I insisted that he did and that he would know what needed to be said at the right time.

The night came when it was his turn to speak. We sang a few campfire songs and then we turned the time to him. "I have given this opportunity to speak a great deal of thought," he began. "Possibly you would be interested in something that happened to me when I was your age."

He continued: "I played on a high-school basketball team, and we made it to the state tournament. On the last night, while we were warming up before the final game, one of the popular girls in the school came down on the gymnasium floor and invited the whole team to her house after the game. We didn't think much about her offer at the time, because the state championship game was only a few moments away. We played the game and won.

"In the locker room afterwards we were deciding what we would do to celebrate, when someone remembered the invitation we had received to go to the home of this girl. So we all went to her house. It turned out that her parents were gone for the weekend. She had rolled back the rug and had invited exactly twelve girls, one for each team member. We went in and sat down in a large circle. The stereo was turned up loud and we were all talking about the game.

"After a while our hostess walked over to the stereo and turned the volume down. 'Listen, fellows,' she said, 'the basketball season is over. You don't need to worry about training any more — you can let your hair down and relax tonight.' Then she pulled out a carton of cigarettes, opened a package, and started it around the circle."

All eyes were on the man telling the story as he went on. "We lived in a Latter-day Saint community. Almost everyone was LDS. Yet as the cigarettes were passed from one to another, every person was taking one. The package was getting closer to me with every second. I didn't want to smoke, but I didn't want to be embarrassed either, by being the exception. I decided to smoke along with the rest.

"By now the cigarettes had reached the fellow next to me. But he merely said 'No, thanks,' and passed them on to me. It was my friend's courage that gave me courage, and I too said 'No, thanks,' and passed the package on."

The storyteller looked intently into the faces lit by the flickering campfire. "My young friends," he said softly, "I have many times wondered what would have happened to me if I had been sitting on the other side of my friend."

Clearly, the person who is the master of self is also the master of situations. He makes decisions based on his own standards and character and not on those of others, whatever the social pressures may be. He does not let the group influence him to do something contrary to his principles.

Total self-mastery is a life-long endeavor, since so many areas of conduct and thought are involved and the temptations and provocations apparently are limitless. Measurably there can be mastery in specific areas early in life, however, and as young Latter-day Saints your strivings need to be geared to that objective. And one of the most important areas in which to make your attack is that wherein many of youth's great struggles for self-mastery occur — control and mastery of the sexual urge.

You've heard many times from various Church speakers that the Lord has put this sex drive in us for a special and glorious purpose in marriage and that its indulgence apart from that set of circumstances is a deep sin. Well, Satan has heard the same speakers, and since "he seeketh that all men might be miserable like unto himself," it is his delight to degrade mankind through this particularly debasing sin.

On Satan's side is the power which this divinely given urge packs *when out of control*. When it comes to resisting the proffered drink or cigarette, it is relatively easy to do so by a rational decision — certainly in the early stages of the situation. But once the sexual urge is allowed to get out of control, as frequently it can do in just seconds, the body and not the mind tends to make the decision. For that reason, too many young Latter-day Saints who would never smoke or drink, who would never think of swearing or telling an off-color story, succumb to temptation and surrender their chastity.

The solution is: *Never take even the first small step in that direction*. If you will observe this rule, the mind and the spirit will always be in control. This means that you should avoid not only the first physical steps but the mental ones too. This is why all of us, youth and adults alike, are continually being cautioned to keep our minds clean; to keep well away from pornography in all its forms and degrees — in fact, from anything that could arouse lewd or suggestive ideas — and to fill our minds with clean and uplifting thoughts. There is no question that self-mastery over our physical appetites requires strong mental self-control; and although perhaps "strong passions accompany great minds," as someone has said, in the continuing conquest of self such emotions must be kept always within bounds.

In modern society there are many who claim that controlling these urges is not only undesirable but impossible. They are wrong on both counts. The Lord's word to the contrary is clear and forthright. It is one of Satan's old lies that this drive has to be satisfied, that we have to seek a release. Young men especially who would like some clarification on this would do well to read the excellent address given by Elder Boyd K. Packer in the priesthood meeting of the October 1976 general conference.

There is a special and wonderful principle built into the human mind and body which is a great aid in controlling the sex drive. It is the principle of sublimation or transmutation. By this principle we can transmute the drive into something constructive, positive, and enriching. In his book, *Think and Grow Rich*, Napoleon Hill has one full chapter on "The Mystery of Sex Transmutation." Let me share a few of his thoughts with you.

"The meaning of the word 'transmute' is, in simple language, 'the changing, or transferring of one element, or form of energy, into another.' . . .Sex transmutation is simple and easily explained. It means the switching of the mind from thoughts of physical expression, to thoughts of some other nature.

"Sex desire is the most powerful of human desires. When driven by this desire, men develop keenness of imagination, courage, will-power, persistence, and creative ability unknown to them at other times.

"The transmutation of sex energy calls for the exercise of will-power, to be sure, but the reward is worth the effort. The desire for sexual expression is inborn and natural. The desire cannot, and should not be submerged or eliminated. But it should be given an outlet through forms of expression which enrich the body, mind, and spirit of man. If not given this form of outlet, through transmutation, it will seek outlets through purely physical channels."

Thus we can and should transmute the sex drive into music, athletics, drama, study, creative writing, and so on, all positive and uplifting expressions. Even more important, as Latter-day Saints we need to transmute this drive into service to our fellowman. The transmutation into service is the reason why missionaries can go on missions for two years and stay clean and pure. They are giving service in the form of teaching people the gospel of Jesus Christ. They are transmuting the sex drive into constructive rather than destructive things.

Learning this lesson of sublimation or transmutation will be of tremendous assistance to you in your quest for self-mastery.

Consider another area of self-mastery. I can best introduce it by some questions which Elder Richard L. Evans once asked.

"If you were choosing someone you had to trust, could you trust yourself? Would you like to meet yourself when you are in trouble? Would you like to be at your own mercy? . . . If there were no . . . courts, no jails, no disgrace — none of the usual fears except your own soul inside of you — would you ever take what you knew you had no right to take? . . . Would you honor an unwritten agreement as honestly as if it were written? If you found a lost article that no one else could possibly know you had found, would you try to return it or would you put it in your own pocket?

"Would you compromise on a question of right or wrong? . . . If you made a mistake, would you admit it or would you pretend to be right even when you knew you were wrong? Could you be trusted as well away from home as you could where you are known? Do you think the world owes you a living or do you honestly know that you should work for what you want? . . . Do you try to get the job done or have you been loafing along for fear you were doing too much?"

When a person answers such questions with complete honesty he is applying one of the significant tests of self-mastery: Am I a person of integrity? Integrity, the firm and complete adherence to the highest moral and ethical standards, is not a common accomplishment. Nevertheless it is an element essential not only to self-mastery but to the life of a true Latter-day Saint.

Integrity implies strict allegiance to an avowed purpose. What is your purpose? Ponder deeply what the Lord would have you do. Read your patriarchal blessing again and remind yourself that the Lord indeed has a work for you to do. How are you going to accomplish that work? Decide what you are willing to sacrifice to accomplish your life's mission. Make your plan. In the broad daylight, when you are thinking clearly, make your decision to do certain things and not to do certain other things. Remember, it must be a firm *decision*, not just a general desire. With the decision made, you will free your mind and heart to cope with larger issues, some of which are unforeseeable at this point. But you won't have to waste energy making over and over again such decisions as whether to attend church regularly, whether to pay tithing and observe the Word of Wisdom, whether to stay clean, and so on.

Important to this firm decision, as we can see from the above comments of Elder Evans, is the area of trust. I recall that, when I was an Explorer Scout, one night I was asked to tend my baby sister. That night the Explorers had a swimming party scheduled. Now, those who knew me as a youth will recall how much I loved swimming. On those wonderful summer days in Salt Lake City I used to go every day with my friends to the Fairmont Park swimming pool. Every day we would swim in at least two different sessions, in boys' plunge and open plunge, and sometimes in addition we would even pick up an evening open plunge. I loved to be in the water.

When the Explorers met on that particular evening and found that I wasn't there, they dropped by the house to see if I would go with them. I told them I couldn't, that I was baby-sitting. They so much wanted me to go with them that they offered to hire a baby-sitter, even to pay my way. Rarely in my life have I wanted anything more ardently than I wanted to go with them that night. I remember their urgings, their pleading and jesting. But I had developed a sense of duty, and I felt bound to the duty at hand. I was firm in my resolve. Finally my friends left. As I went back into the house I experienced the strongest sense of self-control. I had been true to my trust. It was a fulfilling experience.

This loyalty to one's trust, this constant watchfulness to achieve self-mastery, is an assignment from which we can never be released, not even for a moment, not even on vacation or otherwise away from home. It is on such occasions, when we are surrounded by new sights and sounds and are perhaps a little lonely, that we need particularly to be on guard — especially against any temptation to immorality. There have been occasions in my life, as there are in most lives, when I was glad that many years before I had made the decision to be clean, so that the negative answer to the circumstances of the moment was automatic. I strongly urge that every young person make that advance decision.

When you have a fixed course and have made the proper decisions, you have a profound impact on those around you. Decide how much time you are going to allocate to study, determine how much time you are going to spend at work, play, training, practice, etc. Influence your life for good by the decisions you make. You can reasonably foresee and prepare for the types of circumstances you will meet with. Don't let life dish out surprises and temptations which you have not considered and which may throw you off your course.

In this chapter we have discussed only a few of the elements of self-control which lead to self-mastery. There are many others — for example, control of impatience, of temper, of language. Since "the thought is father to the deed," the control of our thoughts is one of the ultimate controls we see. We see these various elements of self-control in people we know. In combination, they appear as self-mastery in every truly great soul.

It will require a lifetime of effort, but you too can gain self-mastery. This is the perfection of which Jesus spoke: "Be ye therefore perfect, even as your Father which is in heaven is perfect." (Matthew 5:48.) As the resurrected Lord, he further clarified this thought. "Therefore, what manner of men ought ye to be? Verily I say unto you, even as I am." (3 Nephi 27:27.)

Even as he is. That is your standard and your objective. The way will not be easy. You will meet many circumstances and people whose influence would deflect you from your course. Don't let them. It's *your* ship, and you can bring her home.

Remember, *you're* at the controls.

4

Two to Honor

Who is your best friend? Who understands you better than anyone else? To whom do you turn when the do-it-yourself project of building *you* gets a bit complicated?

The names of a dozen friends may have come to mind, but have you considered good old mom and dad? Your parents are one of the most valuable tools in your tool chest. They can help you in ways no other tool can. But because we sometimes don't know how to "use" our parents in our building process, we turn to friends for help and advice. Friends are wonderful, an indispensable part of our lives, but relying on them is sometimes rather like using a regular screwdriver when a Phillips screwdriver is much more efficient.

If your parents are a tool which you have not yet effectively learned to "use," I challenge you to improve your relationship with them. Make them your closest and best friends. To do so, you must make clear in your mind one very important distinction. *Your parents may not love what you do, but they will always love you.*

I once spoke at a stake conference on the subject of improving relationships with our children. After the meeting a father came up to me and said: "You have changed my life. I have not had a decent relationship with my son in many years. I'm going to write you and tell you about it." A few days later I received this letter:

"Dear Bishop Featherstone:

"You probably don't recall the brief conversation we had on the stand at the stake center last Saturday night. I told you I had a seventeen-year-old son to whom I haven't spoken a kind word in nine years. He has caused his mother and me many hours of heartbreak, especially in the last two years. He and I haven't had a father-son relationship in over half his life. Isn't that a frightening thought? The little unhappiness he has caused us, however, is nothing compared to the lonely hours he must have spent because of all those years and many nights he went to bed feeling so unloved and unwanted.

"I used to react so violently to his slightest misstep. It had reached the point where he could do nothing right in my eyes, even when he tried. I have even uttered the words, 'I detest him.' Can you imagine?

"When I got home Saturday night, I sat him on the couch and told him how sorry I was for the last nine years. I told him that I love him dearly because he is my son, regardless of what he may have done. I told him that some day he will discover the value of the precious gift of his priesthood and I would be proud to ordain him an elder.

"Wherever he may go, whatever he may do, though his actions cost me what little I have in worldly goods, all I will be able to say to him now is 'I love you, my precious son.' "

Regardless of what you may do, or fail to do, first recognize that your parents do love you.

Second, realize that when parents first become parents, they have not had any experience. The curtain rises on the biggest production of their lives without a single rehearsal. The responsibility of raising children is a building project of tremendous proportions.

With any project you build you generally have a step-by-step instruction sheet. If you're assembling a model airplane, your instruction sheet tells you to attach the wings to the body at slot A before inserting the tail into slot B, and so on. If you're baking a cake, the recipe instructs you to first cream the butter and sugar, then add the eggs. If you're making a dress, the guide sheet tells you the exact sequence to follow in assembling the fabric pieces.

Parents have guidelines too in their project of raising you. They have the scriptures, the advice from a modern-day prophet and apostles, and the benefit of excellent programs offered by the Church. But parents are left on their own to interpret these guidelines; applying these principles becomes a matter of judgment. Raising children is not as routine as assembling an airplane or baking a cake. Parents are without a precise step-by-step blueprint from which to make every day-to-day decision.

You have an obligation to obey your parents whether or not you may agree with them, but realize that no one knows everything about everything. As parents we are trying desperately to learn how to be parents. Our best guidesheet for making day-to-day decisions is experience itself. Someone has said, "By the time you get a little experience as parents, you are usually unemployed." How true that is! I am grateful for an experience I had some years ago which has helped me learn my important responsibilities as a parent.

When my son Scott was nine years of age, one evening my wife and I were preparing to go on an anniversary date. Just as we were ready to leave, Scott stopped me and asked, "Dad, can I please have a dollar?"

I was about to say no, and then I thought for a minute and said: "Well, yes, Scott. I'll give you a dollar if you'll do the dishes tonight so your mother doesn't have to do them when she gets home after our anniversary date. But they must be done right."

I turned to leave. "Dad, can I have the dollar?" Scott again asked.

"You know our deal around here, Scott. You do the dishes, I inspect the job. If it's done right, then I'll pay you the dollar. If it's not, then you do the job until it is done right, then you can be paid. No, you can't have the dollar."

"Dad, I want the dollar!" Scott petitioned, in such a voice that I felt I had been mentally overpowered. I didn't want to, but I reached into my pocket and pulled out a dollar and gave it to him. And then I resented the fact that he had mentally overpowered me.

"All right, you little beggar, here's your dollar. But boy,

those dishes had better be done when we get back, and they had better be done right!" I was a little abusive.

A third time I turned to walk away when Scott stopped me, "Dad, can I go to the drugstore?"

"Scott, do you know what a miracle is?" I asked. "A miracle is for you to take that dollar and put it in your pocket, do the dishes, go downstairs to bed, hang up your pants, and in the morning get up, put your pants on, reach your hand in the pocket and find the dollar is still there. That's a miracle at our house. No, you cannot go to the drugstore. It's dark outside and we'll not have you going down the street in the dark."

My wife and I went outside and climbed into the car. We backed out of the driveway; I turned on the headlights and started down the street. Way down the street, in the darkness where the headlights were penetrating, I saw a boy running lickety-split. I said to Merlene, "That boy runs just like Scott."

"It is Scott," she said. I slammed on the brakes and the tires squealed.

Merlene rolled down the window and I said: "Scott, where are you going? You're going to the drugstore, aren't you?"

Scott immediately burst into tears, and to my wife tears constitute total repentance. From that point on she kicked my leg after everything I said. I told Scott that he should not have disobeyed me, that we did not want him out in the street, and that he had better do those dishes right. And again I was a little abusive.

When my leg was sore enough from my wife kicking my ankle, I said, "All right, Scott, you go to the drugstore, but boy, the dishes had better be done when we get home, and they'd better be done right." Still never having said a word and still crying, he went down one street to the drugstore and we went down another street to go out on our anniversary date.

Merlene was very quiet. Finally I said: "Honey, let's not let this incident spoil our evening. We don't have many evenings together. If Scott has done the dishes when I get home, I'll apologize." We went out and had a lovely time.

About midnight we returned home. You can always tell when we've been away; there's a huge aura of light around the house. Every light was on! We pulled into the driveway, I helped my wife out of the car, and we walked up on the back porch together and into the kitchen. All the dishes were washed and put away, the drainboards and sinks were immaculate, the floor was sparkling clean. The kitchen was spotless and everything was in its place. Then I looked over on the kitchen table and saw it — a present, crudely wrapped in gift paper. Scott had taken a piece of paper out of his school notebook and had written: "Dear Mom and Dad — You're the greatest parents in the world. I love you more than I can say. Have a happy anniversary. Love, Scott."

I felt like the world's biggest dope. I said to my wife, "I don't deserve to open it; you open it." She quickly unwrapped the gift which he had bought. It was a box of chocolates. Scott had left the price tag on — it cost ninety-seven cents plus tax.

"I'm not going to sleep very well tonight," I said. "I've got to go downstairs and see Scott."

The hall light cast a shaft of light on that tow-headed little kid lying on the pillow. I walked over and looked at him for a long moment, and then I said, "Hey, Scott."

Scott sat bolt upright in bed, expecting the worst. "I want you to know what a fine little heart you have and what a fine thing it was you did. I love you. You deserve a better dad than I. You have such a good, kind heart. I want you to know I apologize. Will you please forgive me?"

"Aw, sure, Dad," he said as he reached up and kissed me on the cheek. Then he dropped his head back on the pillow and fell back to sleep like a child with a clean conscience.

After my wife and I had said our evening prayers, we climbed into bed. But I didn't sleep very well. I'm not insensitive to people, I thought. At church I try to watch for the widow who needs someone to talk to or shake hands with, or to pat her gently on the back. I watch for children who are too bashful to even look up from the floor. I try to be aware of people's needs. I try to be sensitive and have empathy. Yet in my own home where it matters most, I am the least sensitive. I made a vow that night that I never again would be insensitive to my children.

So as you attempt to improve your relationship with your parents, realize that we as parents do sometimes make mistakes, but we are only trying to do what appears to be the right thing. Sometimes our vision is narrow, but continue to support us, obey us, and forgive us when we are wrong. We love you. You are more precious than rubies to us, more precious even than our own lives.

I once heard a story about a medieval city which was encircled by the enemy for many days. Their food and water had been cut off and supplies were running low. Finally the besieged sought for terms of surrender.

"Bring your most priceless gems to the gates of the city tomorrow at sunrise," was the reply.

The next morning the gates of the city were opened and out marched thousands of boys and girls — truly the citizens' most priceless possessions.

This story no doubt is fictitious, but its message is certainly true.

The third point to remember is to view parent-child relationships in the proper perspective. A local newspaper ran a picture of a prominent government official holding in his arms a beautiful three-year-old child. The child was blond and radiated a cheerful, happy countenance. But in reality this child was a leukemia sufferer. His days were numbered. What do you suppose his parents taught him, knowing he had only a few weeks to live? Would not their perspective be more acute than other parents'?

It is easy for all of us to lose our proper perspective at times. As parents we erroneously believe that we have an indefinite length of time in which to teach our children and in which to develop a relationship with them. But if we knew that our child had only a few weeks to live we wouldn't worry so much about whether or not he dressed properly all of the time, whether he ate his meals regularly or not, or how clean his room might be. A parent's interest would immediately turn to those things which have eternal implications. We would be very concerned about love and integrity. We would be concerned about teaching you charity, honesty, morality, virtue. We would be concerned that we teach you how to become pure in heart, to strive to become more spiritual, to have mental and physical ambition, and so forth. We would let you know that you are vitally important, especially to us, your parents, and we would be more aware of the many mute signs you give constantly to us, letting us know of your need for someone to sincerely care.

Conversely, if you knew you had a limited amount of time to

spend with your parents, would not your perspective change? Instead of complaining about your responsibilities in your home, wouldn't you try to do everything possible to make your parents' burden lighter? You wouldn't stay out late or conduct yourself in any way which would cause your parents undue worry or concern. You would want to dress in such a manner, do your school work and attend your Church meetings so as to make your parents proud of you and happy that you carry their name.

I recall a story of a family which lived on a farm several miles from town. It was autumn and the family had worked particularly hard one day harvesting hay. Steven, the seventeen-year-old son, was unusually tired and anxious to stack the last bale of hay so that he could relax. Finally the hay was all neatly stored. As father and son walked toward the house, Steven's father said: "I'm sorry to have to ask you, but would you please drive into town and pick up the replacement part for the tractor. We'll need it tomorrow so we can plow the north field."

Steve felt annoyance and frustration rising within him. He thought: "Why do I have to go? I've worked hard all day and I'm exhausted." But as he looked at the older man's face he could see fatigue there too. He controlled his feelings, climbed into the truck, and headed for town.

When Steven returned home nearly two hours later, he was surprised to see the bishop's car in front of the house. Several neighbors were at the door. Inside Steve learned that during his absence his father had suffered a heart attack and had passed away. In the great sorrow of that moment, how grateful Steve was that he had resisted the impulse to complain! How glad he was that he had carried out his father's last request!

Finally, as you make a conscientious effort to improve your relationship with your parents, remember that the Lord has instituted a marvelous program for your benefit — the family home evening program. You have a responsibility to make family home evening a meaningful experience.

As the patriarch, your father will preside over and often conduct family home evenings; or he may choose to assign this responsibility to another member of the family. But it takes total family participation to make family home evening as special as the Lord would have it be. Participate by singing the hymns which are selected and by reading the scriptures. If you're called upon to give a lesson, study it and prepare for it as you would if you were giving a Sunday School class lesson. Be interested in the discussions. Be a participating member of the family. And never complain, quarrel with your brothers or sisters, or have a negative attitude.

Some time ago, just prior to my call as a General Authority, I was a stake president in the Boise area. I recall that one Saturday night at a stake conference the congregation were singing "Come, Come, Ye Saints." We started singing the third verse: "We'll find a place which God for us prepared, / Far away in the West, / Where none can come to hurt or make afraid; / There the Saints will be blessed." As we sang, tears started streaming down my cheeks. I thought of the drug problems, the immorality, the peddlers of filth and pornographic materials, and I thought, "Dear God, why isn't there a place in our generation where we can go where none can come to hurt or make afraid?" And just as clearly as anything has ever come to me by way of inspiration, the words came into my mind, "My son, there is — family home evening." Every member of the Church can find a haven of peace and quiet, a haven of peace and protection, if they will but faithfully hold family home evening.

In conclusion, remember, my friends, that your parents are one of the greatest tools for your development you will ever have. Honor and obey them. They will never ask you to do anything that is wrong. Sometimes they may be mistaken and make poor decisions, or they may give incorrect judgment on the basis of partial facts, but they will not deliberately direct you to do anything that is wrong. They are trying to bless your life. It will be a blessing to you to obey them, to conform to their counsel, to follow them as the Lord would have you do.

In the majority of active families in the Church, every prayer that a parent offers, morning, noon or night, in secret or with others, contains an expression asking the Lord to watch over and bless his or her children. You are the most priceless possessions we have. Make every effort to understand your parents, to try and follow them in righteousness. And if you by chance have a parent who is not righteous, you do not have to follow him or her to do evil. Choose to be something better and something more noble, to live up to the divine nature which the Lord has placed in you.

May you truly develop a close relationship with your parents. Learn to communicate with them, and they will become a valuable tool in building *you*.

5

The Outer
Cover

When you decide to get out of bed in the morning, what makes you move? (I'm not referring to your mother or to your alarm clock!) What happens inside you that impels you up off the mattress and onto your feet? What physical force enables you to put on your slippers, stumble to the breakfast table, and spoon your cereal from the bowl to your mouth?

The answers to these questions are all the same. Between your brain and your muscles is a remarkable stimulus-response circuit called your nervous system. When your brain decides it's time to get your body out of bed, it sends an impulse through the nervous system. Each neuron or nerve cell is connected to muscle tissue. The impulse stimulates the neurons which cause the muscles to react and boost you from your bed. An impulse from your brain travels through your nervous system at the rate of two hundred miles per hour, activating the muscles which enable you to move.

Isn't it wonderful to be able to make our bodies respond to our every command, to be in complete and absolute control over them! Whether we're swimming, an activity which requires the coordination of many muscles and many movements, or just winking an eye, the movement is literally "no sooner *thought* than done."

It is a great blessing to have control over our physical bodies. Unfortunately, not everyone does. Sometimes there is a breakdown in this remarkable stimulus-response circuit. Many thousands of stroke and accident victims suffer from paralysis. No matter how hard their minds may think "move," their bodies cannot respond to the command. The same is true of many who are born with or contract cerebral palsy, muscular dystrophy, polio, and other crippling diseases. These unfortunate victims would give all they have just to exercise complete control over their physical bodies. But usually through no fault of their own they have lost this marvelous ability.

There is another group of people who have lost this ability, but not through heredity, birth defect, or by accident. These people have lost control over their physical bodies by *choice* instead of *chance*. These people have willfully submitted their bodies to the control of foreign substances such as alcohol, drugs, tobacco and habit-forming beverages. What a great privilege they have forsaken in exchange for a few "worldly pleasures"! Willful submission to these intoxicating substances has deprived them of their most valuable possession — free agency. This freedom consists of the ability "to act for themselves and not be acted upon." (2 Nephi 2:26.) If we allow our bodies to be ruled by drugs, alcohol, and the like, are we acting for ourselves or being acted upon? Do we have complete control over our actions, or does something else? Do we really have our free agency? Some Church members and many investigators to the Church argue that the Word of Wisdom limits their free agency. But just the opposite is true. Obedience to the Word of Wisdom actually increases our free agency — it enhances our ability to act for ourselves rather than be acted upon.

The Word of Wisdom was given by revelation to the Prophet Joseph Smith in 1833. It contains both positive and negative instructions regarding the care of our bodies. It is only right that the Lord should instruct us in the proper care of our bodies. When we purchase a new appliance it is expected that it will be accompanied by a set of instructions. The manufacturer of the product tells us how to best use the product and how to care for it to ensure longest life and maximum use.

The Word of Wisdom is a set of instructions from our Maker on how to care for and keep ourselves fit for the purpose for which we were created. When it was first given it was given by way of instruction, but it has since been made a commandment. In this chapter I will deal only with those things we are commanded not to take into our bodies because these represent the greatest danger to your generation.

Three types of things are specifically prohibited by the Word of Wisdom — strong drinks, tobacco, and hot drinks. There are other substances which have a harmful effect on the human body, though they are not specifically prohibited by the Word of Wisdom. Cola drinks and harmful drugs of any sort are in violation of the spirit of the Word of Wisdom. Let's look at each of these substances separately to better understand why we have been cautioned against their use.

The Doctrine and Covenants tells us: "That inasmuch as any man drinketh wine or strong drink among you, behold it is not good, neither meet in the sight of your father. . . . And, again, strong drinks are not for the belly, but for the washing of your bodies." (D&C 89:5,7.)

The Lord spoke in language common to the people living at the time this revelation was given. The meaning was plain and clear — alcohol in any combination or mixture is injurious to the body when taken internally, but may be good for external application. In 1833 when the revelation was given, the ordinary name for beverages containing alcohol was "strong drinks," thus the caution to abstain from alcoholic beverages was very explicit.

You need only to look at a few statistics to see that this revelation was divinely inspired and given to us for our own good. Alcohol is responsible for over thirty thousand highway deaths each year. One-half of all traffic fatalities have significant amounts of alcohol in their blood. Over 60 percent of the teenage highway deaths are attributable to alcohol as a major cause. Alcohol abuse and alcoholism cost our economy over fifteen billion dollars a year, and it shortens the life span of every user by ten to twelve years. What a tremendous waste!

President McKay used to quote a verse entitled "It's Nobody's Business" which went like this:

It's nobody's business what I drink.
I care not what my neighbors think,
Or how many laws they choose to pass,
I'll tell the world I have my glass.
Here one man's freedom could not be curbed,
His right to drink was undisturbed,
So he drank in spite of law or man,
And jumped inside his old tin can.
He stepped on the gas and let her go,
Down the highway to and fro.
He hit the curves at fifty miles,
With bleary eyes and drunken smiles.
Not long till a car he tried to pass,
There was a crash, a scream and breaking glass,
And the other car was upside down,
About ten miles to the nearest town.
And the man was free, but his wife was caught.
And she needed the help of that drunken sot,
Who sat in a fogged and drunken daze,
And heard the scream and saw the blaze,
But was too far gone to save a life,
By helping the car from off the wife.
Now the car was burned and the mother died,
And a husband wept and a baby cried
And a drunk sat by, and still some think,
It's nobody's business what they drink.

Statistics reflect a grim picture in terms of the loss of money and lives caused by alcohol. But no one will ever be able to compute the damage alcohol has caused in terms of dishonesty, infidelity, broken homes and ruined lives. I know from first-hand experience what a life of misery alcohol can cause. My father was an alcoholic. I know what it is like to have bill collectors pounding at the door and no money to pay them because it was all spent on alcohol. I know what it is like not to have any food in the home. I know what it is like to go to school in ridiculous, embarrassing clothes because there was not money to purchase anything better. I know what it is like to have constant contention, quarreling, arguing and fighting in the home between parents. I know what misery alcohol can bring.

As Latter-day Saint youth you must make a firm commitment to yourself that you will obey the Word of Wisdom. I am sure there are many temptations before you to do otherwise. Because of curiosity many youth your age are experimenting with alcohol. Alcoholic beverages are frequently passed around at football and basketball games, and there is much social pressure to participate. To avoid this problem, if possible attend athletic games with those of your own faith, those who have the same high standards and determination to live the commandments which you do. There is a great temptation on high school graduation day. Friends may encourage you to join them and "live it up." But don't. Stand firm in your beliefs. Make your decision right now that you will keep the Word of Wisdom, that you will never take that first drink. Then you will avoid having to make that decision over and over every time the opportunity presents itself. And once you have firmly and resolutely made up your mind, the temptation will be considerably lessened.

The Word of Wisdom continues to caution us: "And again, tobacco is not for the body, neither for the belly, and is not good for man, but is an herb for bruises and all sick cattle, to be used with judgment and skill." (D&C 89:8.)

When the Prophet Joseph Smith received this revelation there was no scientific evidence to support abstinence from tobacco. In the past few years, however, three hazardous substances have been found in cigarette smoke — tobacco "tar," nicotine, and carbon monoxide. Tobacco tar, which is collected by condensing tobacco smoke, has been found to contain several cancer-producing substances. Nicotine is a potent and habit-forming drug which stimulates the central nervous system, the heart, and other body systems. Carbon monoxide, which is produced by the incomplete burning of organic material, passes into the blood of smokers and acts as a poison by reducing the amount of oxygen available to cells in the body.

These three harmful substances have been shown to cause coronary artery disease, chronic bronchitis, emphysema, and lung cancer. Yet in spite of the numerous government and private-industry reports declaring the ill effects of cigarette smoking, teenagers are taking up smoking at an increasing rate. Why? What possible advantage can there be in acquiring this dirty, distasteful, harmful habit?

President N. Eldon Tanner tells of an experience he had while driving in his car with two young men. "A young man thumbed a ride with us. I asked the boys that were with me if we should take him with us and they said yes.

"I picked him up, and after we had driven a little way he said, 'Do you mind if I smoke in your car?'

"I said, 'No, not at all, if you can give me any good reason why you should smoke.' And I said, 'I will go farther than that.' (I was a stake president at this time.) 'If you can give me a good reason why you should smoke, I will smoke with you.'

"Well, these two young men looked at me and wondered. We drove on for some distance, about twenty minutes, I think, and I turned and said:

" 'Aren't you going to smoke?'

"And he said, 'No.'

"I said, 'Why not?'

" 'I can't think of a good reason why I should.' "

There is not a good reason why you should smoke either, but there are plenty of good reasons why you should not. Besides the detrimental effects it has on our bodies, smoking is a terrible waste of money.

I once heard a story about a young married couple who began setting up housekeeping. Their budget was extremely limited and their furnishings few. The wife, attempting to stretch the budget and furnish the house with a few modest purchases each month, repeatedly asked her husband to give up his expensive smoking habit. When he repeatedly refused to do so, she announced that she planned to spend a similar amount on herself. She purchased a little piggy bank and dropped into it everyday the price of a package of cigarettes. When her husband was unusually nervous and smoked more than one package, she doubled the amount. Her husband said that the money he spent on cigarettes was negligible, that her savings would never amount to anything, but she kept on saving.

Several years later, during the height of the depression of the 1930s, he came home one evening to find a baby grand piano in the living room. Immediately he began to scold, reminding her that the country was in a serious depression and that his salary had been reduced. She calmly replied: "Don't get excited. It's all paid for. I bought it with my cigarette money."

The husband was skeptical. He sat down with paper and pencil and soon had to admit that she had purchased a real bargain with her cigarette money, his having gone up in smoke. He resolved to quit his expensive habit, but he could not. He had become a slave to it.

Several more years passed. One day the wife announced that she was going to Europe the following summer. The husband reminded her that they could not afford such a trip. Again she calmly replied: "You can't afford it, but I can. I'm going on my cigarette money!"

Besides being a terrible waste of money and detrimental to our physical well-being, smoking also has an effect on our spiritual welfare. When a young Latter-day Saint takes up smoking he no longer feels comfortable around other Latter-day Saints who keep the Word of Wisdom. Instead he seeks new friends who have similar standards. Subtle Satan tells him: "You're no longer welcome around Latter-day Saints. They can smell cigarette smoke on your clothes and on your breath. But don't worry. Smoking is a minor offense. Other Latter-day Saints have worse vices which have no distinguishable odors, such as dishonesty and immorality. Go ahead and smoke and just find other friends. Come with me."

In this way Latter-day Saint youths are led into undesirable crowds. The Spirit of the Lord withdraws from them and they are left to the temptations of Satan, who proceeds to draw them into even more serious transgressions.

Many years ago the *New York Observer* ran a clever little article which sums up the evils of smoking: "I am not much of a mathematician," said the cigarette, "but I can add to a man's nervous troubles, I can subtract from his physical energy, I can multiply his aches and pains, I can divide his mental powers, I take interest from his work, and discount his chances for success." How true that is! How grateful we should be for a loving Father in heaven who has cautioned us against this evil!

"And again, hot drinks are not for the body or belly." (D&C 89:9.) Hyrum Smith, brother of the Prophet Joseph Smith, explained the meaning of the term "hot drinks": "There are many who wonder what this can mean — whether it refers to tea, or coffee, or not. I say it does refer to tea and coffee."

Tea and coffee contain caffeine, which is a stimulant and can be most habit-forming. In addition, medical science has found that excessively hot drinks interfere with the digestive processes and may cause injury to the stomach. Yet these consequences seem relatively innocent compared with the obvious detrimental effects of alcohol and tobacco. But remember that at the time the Word of Wisdom was given no one could see any harm in tobacco. The Lord loved his Saints enough to caution them against these things, even though, at the time, the world could find no danger in them. I am sure the same is true today of tea and coffee. Medical science is now finding more and more reasons which substantiate the Word of Wisdom. How fortunate we are to have received this special health knowledge a century and a half before the rest of the world!

Strong drinks, tobacco, and hot drinks are the three "don'ts" specifically mentioned in the Word of Wisdom. But the Doctrine and Covenants also tells us: "For behold, it is not meet that I should command in all things; for he that is compelled in all things, the same is a slothful and not a wise servant; wherefore he receiveth no reward." (D&C 58:26.) In keeping with the spirit of the Word of Wisdom, we are wise servants if we avoid any substance which is harmful to our bodies, whether or not it is explicitly mentioned. Two such substances are cola beverages and drugs.

In February of 1972 the Church issued a statement in the Priesthood Bulletin regarding cola drinks: "The Word of Wisdom, section 89 of the Doctrine and Covenants, remains as to terms and specifications as found in that section. There has been no official interpretation of that Word of Wisdom except that which was given by the Brethren in the very early days of the Church when it was declared that 'hot drinks' meant tea and coffee.

"With reference to cola drinks, the Church has never officially taken a position on this matter, but the leaders of the Church have advised, and we do now specifically advise, against the use of any drink containing harmful, habit-forming drugs under circumstances that would result in acquiring the habit. Any beverage that contains ingredients harmful to the body should be avoided."

Can cola beverages really be addictive? Yes. They contain caffeine, the same substance found in tea and coffee. It can be very habit-forming. A friend of mine knew a young man who drank a minimum of six bottles of cola every day, usually more. The back porch of his home was a sea of empty bottles. My friend had an occasion to travel by bus with this young man on a school outing. When the bus made a rest stop most of the members of the group purchased a 7-Up or root beer from the soda fountain, but this young man headed for the nearest grocery store and bought a six-pack of cola. He had become so addicted to the beverage that he had to have a cola in order to feel well. What happened to his free agency? Who was really in control over his physical body?

Avoid cola beverages and other soft drinks which contain caffeine. There are many other soft drinks available which are not nearly so detrimental to our health. Let's live by the spirit of the Word of Wisdom and by the counsel given in the Priesthood Bulletin. Let's refrain from drinking cola beverages and enjoy better physical and spiritual health.

Lastly, there is the matter of drugs. Whether prescribed or obtained via patent medicines, far too many drugs are poured down far too many throats in efforts to alleviate physical ills. With our knowledge of the importance of the human body, Latter-day Saints should be extremely careful about the use of drugs for any reason at all. Particularly they should totally abstain from drug abuse, from what we call the "drug scene."

Television programs and movies are flooded with stories of drug users, and it is not surprising that many youth desire to know first-hand what these experiences are like. They may report that a drug trip is wonderful, a marvelous thrill. But if someone told you that the ultimate thrill you could ever experience was free falling through the air, would you be foolish enough to jump off a tall building to experience it? You would know that the price of a crash landing a few hundred feet below is too high a price to pay for a momentary thrill. And so it is with drugs.

I have interviewed potential missionaries who have been the drug route, who sought that fabulous thrill. One such missionary I interviewed told me that he had not taken drugs for over a year, yet six months after his last encounter he experienced a relapse. He was sent to a hospital psychiatric ward where he received intensive psychiatric treatment. "For two weeks I actually thought I was a dog," the young man related. "There wasn't any question about it. I wasn't being smart or trying to be funny. I actually believed that I was a dog." What a high price he paid for his momentary thrill!

Some drug advocates argue that drugs relieve them of all their pressures and anxieties. Everyone has problems and pressures, and at one time or another everyone has wished that his difficulties would disappear. But the Lord intended that we have problems, that we grow and mature by facing and solving our problems and not running away from them. Problems are a necessary part of our lives and we must learn to meet them, not escape them through drugs.

Don't be fooled by the advice of those who argue the merits of drugs. The world is full of crazy people who would have you believe some pretty crazy things. For example, during World War II the Japanese recruited kamikaze pilots — pilots who were willing to dive their planes headlong into enemy ships in order to ensure a direct hit. A group of newly recruited kamikazes was called into an emergency session by their captain. "Honorable kamikaze pilots," the leader began, "take airplanes, fly high in the sky, find enemy ships, dive planes into ships, blow up enemy, die for glorious emperor." In the far corner of the room sat a young Japanese man who, when the leader finished speaking, muttered an observation shared by many, "Captain, you are crazy as a bed bug."

The idea was indeed crazy, yet this leader still had followers. No matter how crazy an idea, someone is always willing to fall for it. There is no intelligent or rational reason for you to take drugs; it is a crazy idea. Don't you be foolish enough to fall for it.

Some youths would never think of experimenting with LSD, marijuana, or heroin but instead misuse over-the-counter and prescription drugs such as diuretics, sleeping pills, and pain killers. These are as much in violation of the spirit of the Word of Wisdom as are more illegal narcotics. They prohibit our bodies from functioning properly and can have a most damaging effect on our physical and mental well-being. Take these drugs only as prescribed.

Ewart A. Swinyard had this to say about the harmful effects of drug misuse. He began by quoting a passage from Harold B. Lee's book *Decisions for Successful Living* (Deseret Book Company, 1973, page 97): "One of the most scenic drives in the state of Arizona is through Oak Creek Canyon that lies between Flagstaff and Jerome. To enter the canyon from Flagstaff the descent is very steep, requiring expert roadbuilders to construct the winding highway, with sharp hairpin turns to get the traveler to the floor of the canyon. Just as with all paths that lead downward, no effort at all is required to go all the way to the bottom; indeed all the going is so easy that unless you apply your brakes at the dangerous turns, you would meet early disaster. When you arrive at Jerome, however, the situation is just reversed. Before you is the sheer wall of the canyon that can only be surmounted by a series of ladder-like roads constructed on ascending levels. What energy or gasoline you think you saved in coming down, you now must expend and more to climb back up."

Dr. Swinyard commented: "The misuse and overuse of over-the-counter remedies, prescription drugs, and almost any drug, is like a trip through Oak Creek Canyon. At first these agents appear to make life easier, to relieve real or imaginary illnesses, but eventually each one of us must pay back whatever we might have gained and face the judgment of God's inexorable law: 'As ye sow, so shall ye reap.'

"God created all things for the use of his children here upon the earth. The development of highly selective and potent drugs is one of the choice blessings he has given to this dispensation. When used wisely, modern drugs prevent disease, prolong life, relieve suffering, and benefit all mankind. When misused or overused, they may induce disease, destroy life, cause untold suffering, and weaken society."

In this chapter we have discussed some of the scientific evidences supportive of the Word of Wisdom. Let me say that we do not know whether science has discovered all the possible harmful effects of the substances concerned. There may be others we don't know about. But God knows. And what is our need to know all the reasons? All we have to do is follow the counsel of a loving Father, the creator of our bodies, who has told us what is best for us in these matters.

Your body, your outer cover, is the most precious possession you own. Satan and his third of the hosts of heaven have no outer cover and they would love to possess yours. I hope you realize just what a marvelous blessing it is to have a body, for if you do, you will not want to do anything which would harm or misuse it in any way.

Primary children used to sing a beautiful little hymn called "My Body Is a Temple." Perhaps you recall the words.

> *My body is a temple*
> *That needs the greatest care;*
> *It must be clean and wholesome*
> *To house my spirit here.*

May the Lord bless you that you will realize what a privilege it is to have a body, an earthly temple for your spirit. May you always keep it clean and wholesome and may you always remain in absolute and complete control over it, your outer cover.

6

The Inner Man

What are you made of? Anatomy books say you are 60 percent water. You have some thirty trillion cells, between five and six quarts of blood, thirty feet of digestive canal, 206 bones, thirty-two teeth (give or take a few!), and a lot more — all under twenty square feet of skin.

But there's something else under that skin. Let's call it "moral fiber." It's not a part of your skeletal, muscular, cardiovascular, nervous or digestive system, but it is very much a part of you. What are you feeding your moral fiber to keep it alive?

You have no doubt heard the expression "you are what you eat." It is very true. Our physical bodies have the ability to synthesize the food we consume, sorting out the amino acids, the vitamins, the carbohydrates, and so on. Portions of yesterday's roast beef sandwich will tomorrow be new bone marrow, red blood cells, skin tissue, and so forth. For maximum health you must feed your body nutritious food, not junk food, for it can only function properly and grow from the ingestion of proper nutrients.

But what about your moral fiber? What have you fed it lately? Just as your body will get sick unless it receives the proper food, your moral fiber or character will become chronically ill if it is fed the wrong type of food.

What type of food builds the inner man? The list of wholesome influences which make a positive contribution to our moral fiber is extensive. So instead let's look at some of the junk foods which do not build our moral fiber — junk to avoid if we are to remain healthy.

Let's first look at the junkiest of all foods — pornography. Just how offensive to our inner character is it? A thesaurus, a book which gives word synonyms, lists these synonyms or related words for pornographic: obscene, lewd, dirty, lurid, smutty, impure, unchaste, unclean, foul, filthy, nasty, vile, offensive, unprintable, foul-mouthed, foul-tongued, foul-spoken, and the list goes on and on.

These words should be enough to tell us that pornography is not healthy food for our moral fiber. But our minds are not like our stomachs. If we feed our stomachs garbage they can regurgitate it and cast it from us. If we feed our minds garbage, however, they can not as easily throw it off. The mind is like a computer which can classify and store great volumes of material. You program it by what you feed into it. Pornographic material will always be in store, and the more often you retrieve it the more damaging will be its effect.

"But what harm will it do?" you may ask. "It's not all that serious. I'm not intending to do those things, I only want to look a little." If you think these thoughts you are the victim of one of Satan's most powerful and effective tools. He wants us to think it is not all that serious. He wants us to think that others are doing it. For he knows that if he can get us just a little bit caught in the wiles of pornography it will increase its hold until we are fast in its grip.

Have you heard of the Rancho LaBrea tar pits in Los Angeles, California? Sticky black tar from subterranean sources has oozed into these pits for centuries. After a rainfall these pits are covered with water and many a thirsty animal has mistaken these pits for refreshing drinking pools. Caught in the shallows of the pits the animals would struggle in vain for freedom and eventually die of starvation. If they leapt into the center of the pit they would be slowly drawn downward to a horrible mass of black tar, suffocation, and death. Tens of thousands of animal bones and thousands of complete skeletons, many of now-extinct species, have been dug from these tar pits.

Pornography is like these deceptive tar pits. Whether we just stand at the edge and drink or leap all the way in, once we are entrapped by pornography it is difficult to free ourselves from its vice. Why? Because pornography has an evil way of stirring up the physical appetites, clouding the mind, and destroying the soul.

Our objective in this life is to comply with the standards and teachings of the gospel of Jesus Christ, to prove faithful, to endure to the end when we will be able to come back into the presence of our Heavenly Father in an exalted state. When we indulge in pornography, cloudiness and gray areas obscure our thinking. Our determination to keep the commandments is lessened, and we no longer have the Holy Ghost to give us an understanding of the truth of all things. The Spirit withdraws from us and we are left to ourselves to reason things out. And as such we are even more inclined toward the prompting of the devil, even more inclined toward evil.

President McKay said, "When we dive to the depth of pleasure we come up with more sand than pearls." There are so many pearls readily available to us, so much good material to assimilate. Why dive for anything more? Spend your leisure time reading wholesome materials — the scriptures, the Church magazines, books by Church authorities, and wholesome literature outside the Church such as enlightening biographies and good novels. Mortal life, the time of preparation, is too short to spend on unproductive and unwholesome activities.

Unfortunately, we are exposed to pornographic materials of some sort nearly every day. But we don't have to let our minds dwell on them. The scriptures repeatedly tell us, "Be ye clean that bear the vessels of the Lord." We cannot purge from our lives thoughts that are impure if we are reading and seeing pornographic materials. Let's throw out this garbage and not let it affect our spiritual health.

What are some other junk foods to be avoided? Certainly gambling is one because of the insidious way it decays our moral fiber. It can be as habit-forming as cigarettes, alcohol, or drugs. So addictive is this vice that every conceivable crime has been committed in pursuit of gambling money. It has driven countless people to suicide and reduced families which should be living comfortably and respectably to lives of poverty and distress. There are thousands and thousands of cases of fathers deserting their families, mothers neglecting their children, wives robbing their husbands of the earnings of months and years, and people pawning all they have in order to indulge in gambling.

Not only does this vice cost dearly in terms of human lives and suffering, but it is a tremendous waste of money. A *U.S. News and World Report* article listed the principal forms of crime in America and the cost per year of each. Gambling led the list, costing over thirty billion dollars per year. Gambling losses were five times the narcotics bill, more than twenty times the cost of hijackings, and four times the losses in embezzlements, fraud and forgery combined. Ten times more money was lost on gambling than in robberies, thefts, burglaries, and shoplifting; twenty-five times more than from vandalism and arson; and twice as much as the cost of maintaining all federal, state and local police forces and operating the United States penal systems and criminal courts.

Robert Kennedy once said: " . . . the American people are spending more on gambling than on medical care or education; . . .in so doing, they are putting up the money for the corruption of public officials and the vicious activities of the dope peddlers, loan sharks, bootleggers, white slave traders, and slick confidence men. Investigation . . .has disclosed without any shadow of a doubt that corruption and racketeering, financed largely by gambling, are weakening the vitality and strength of this nation." (As quoted in *The Ensign*, November 1972, page 43.)

"But that's all big-time gambling," you may say. "What's the harm in a simple penny-ante poker game or a little wager on the World Series?" In answer let me relate a story which comes out of the Old West. The owner of a stage coach company was looking to hire an additional stage coach driver. As he interviewed each prospective candidate he asked, "How close would you say you could drive to the edge of the cliff without going over?"

"Why, I'm so skillful with a team of horses and a stagecoach," boasted the first man, "that I can place the outer wheels less than a foot from the edge of the cliff and still take the curves at top speed without the slightest trouble!"

The second candidate, anxious to outdo the first, bragged: "Oh, that's nothing. I can drive with the outer wheels three inches from the edge of the cliff and round the curves at full speed without going over the edge."

Having heard the first two answers, the third applicant simply said, "I keep as far from the outer edge as possible."

It is needless to say which man was hired for the job.

The same is true with gambling. The penny-ante poker game or a little wager on the World Series seems innocent enough, but how close to the edge of the cliff can you get before falling off? Little vices get bigger and bigger and we get closer and closer to the edge of the cliff.

As members of the Church we have been strongly admonished to "keep as far from the outer edge as possible." We have been cautioned against any act that risks something of value on the outcome of an event which is determined in part or entirely by chance. President Heber J. Grant set forth the following statement in 1925: "The Church has been and now is unalterably opposed to gambling in any form whatever. It is opposed to any game of chance, occupation, or so-called business, which takes money from the person who may be possessed of it without giving value received in return."

This very clearly excludes betting on horse or dog races and athletic competitions. It rules out slot machines and gambling tables of every sort. And raffles and lotteries in which a person purchases a chance at winning a prize are also forms of gambling.

The Church has cautioned us against gambling because it weakens our moral fiber. One of Satan's clever tools is to make us think we are getting something for nothing — or next to nothing. I heard a statement many years ago which I have found to be very true: "There ain't no such thing as a free lunch." The person who persists in gambling loses something far more valuable than his money — he loses his high ethics of work, industry, thrift and service, the very principles which have made our Church and our country strong. Instead they are replaced with the hopes of getting something without effort, something without paying the full price.

Gambling is also an extraordinary waste of time. There is nothing physically, intellectually or spiritually profitable about it. And because it can be so addictive, thousands of people not only indulge all their free time in it, but neglect their work and family responsibilities in favor of gambling. Richard L. Evans of the Council of the Twelve said: "The spirit of gambling is a progressive thing. Usually it begins modestly; and then, like many other hazardous habits, it often grows beyond control. At best it wastes time and produces nothing. At worst it becomes a ruinous obsession and fosters false living by encouraging the futile belief that we can continually get something for nothing."

But let me tell you the most important reason to avoid gambling. The reason is that it is inconsistent with the companionship of the Holy Spirit. Gambling dulls the spiritual sensitivities. With the adversary alert to destroy your moral fiber, he would be delighted to have you to think that life is nothing but chance — a big gamble — and that it doesn't matter what you do. But the purpose of this book is to help you see that it does matter, to help you realize what your destiny can be, and to guide you in setting goals and objectives to help you build your destiny. It is a plan that requires determination, self-discipline, hard work, and the help of the Lord — not luck.

We are blessed to belong to the church of Jesus Christ, to know that we have a loving and kind Heavenly Father who by design and by plan provided a way by which we can come back into his presence. We should not want to ever put ourselves in a situation which would interfere with that plan. Let's make up our minds, once and for all, that there are some things which we will not do — and one of them is gambling. Let's not take any risks which would limit our opportunities to develop and improve ourselves and make our way back into the exaltation of the Lord.

A third junk food which is closely associated with gambling is card playing. Many members of the Church can see no harm in playing cards if gambling is not involved. I can see two very important reasons to avoid filling our lives with this junk food. First, card playing can be addictive, and second, it is an extraordinary waste of time.

Elder John A. Widtsoe strongly criticized card playing: "It has been observed through centuries of experience that the habit of card playing becomes fixed upon a person and increases until he feels that a day without a game of cards is incomplete. After an afternoon or evening at card-playing, nothing has been changed, no new knowledge, thoughts, or visions have come, no new hopes or aspirations have been generated, except for another opportunity to waste precious hours. It leads nowhere; it is a dead-end road. . . ." (As quoted in *The Ensign*, November 1972, page 47.)

I knew of a young man who thoroughly enjoyed playing cards but seldom participated because of the pressures of his work and the many demands upon his time. He did indulge his fancy at Christmastime, however, when he visited his family out of state. Nearly every night during the holidays was spent playing hearts, bridge, or some other card game. When he returned home after the holidays the card-playing fever was in his blood, and in spite of the increased business demands due to his absence, he would take every opportunity to play a game of cards.

The Church strongly disapproves of face cards and of any game that involves face cards, even though it is not a game of gambling. Have the courage to comply with the standards of the Church on this matter. I remember many years ago when I was a Scout that several of the young men brought face cards on Scout outings. They spent much time playing cards. Yet there was an immense variety of other things to do, places to go, wholesome games to play for entertainment. This is even more true today.

You may be invited to an outing or a party where the entire evening is spent playing cards. Do you have the courage to stand up for what you believe? Could you simply say, "I'd rather not"? You do not need to argue whether playing cards is right or wrong, simply say that you would rather not join in the game but that you will find other pleasant things to do at the party.

If you can exhibit this type of courage, people will respect you for your integrity, the Lord will bless you for your willingness to keep his commandments and do what is right, and your moral fiber will remain strong and healthy.

These junk foods which I have discussed are habits that

affect the mind and the soul. Let's examine one more junk food, one more particularly vicious habit — profanity.

Language which is vulgar and leaves an impression of uncleanliness and unwholesomeness is not in keeping with the gospel of Jesus Christ, neither is language which is irreverent or contemptuous of holy things. But the most wicked of all profanity is that which blasphemes the name of Deity. Joseph Fielding Smith said: "Above all else we should hold the name of Deity in the most sacred and solemn respect. Nothing is so distressing or shocks the feelings of a refined person more than to hear some uncouth, ignorant, or filthy creature, bandy around the name of Deity."

Yet how often each day do we hear such language! And how easy it is to adopt this vocabulary if we do not make a consistent effort to avoid it! Don't permit yourself to say even that first profane word because the first profane utterance makes it easier to swear again and again. Profanity isn't cute or clever, and it doesn't make us appear bigger in the eyes of our peers. It only degrades us. It only tells others what we are really like inside. It is an evidence of a sick moral fiber.

A gym instructor, tired of hearing so much profanity in his gymnasium, wrote ten reasons why every respectable person should swear. Rather than verbally reprimanding the users of profanity he quietly handed each offender these ten reasons:

"Ten good reasons why every respectable thinking man should swear just as often and as hard as he can:

"1. Because it is such an elegant way of expressing one's thoughts.

"2. Because it is such a conclusive proof of taste and good breeding.

"3. Because it is such a sure way of making one's self agreeable to his friends.

"4. Because it is a positive evidence of acquaintance with good literature.

"5. Because it furnishes such a good example and training for boys.

"6. Because it is just what a man's mother enjoys having her son do.

"7. Because it would look so nice in print.

"8. Because it is such a good way of increasing one's self-respect.

"9. Because it is such a help to manhood and virtue in many ways.

"10. Because it is such an infallible way of improving one's chances in the hereafter."

Profanity is junk food which is totally void of food value. It is as offensive to our Heavenly Father as it is to our moral fiber. Don't permit it to poison your soul.

All of these junk foods deteriorate our moral fiber. They are indirect tools of the devil, designed to weaken our moral values and make us less subject to the promptings of the Spirit and more subject to the enticings of the adversary. We must cautiously avoid them.

Even more direct tools of the devil are the various spirit mediums. Many youth today are experimenting with Ouija boards, "up table," and other spiritualistic games. These games are often conducted in dimly lit rooms. Remember that another of Satan's names is the Prince of Darkness and such an environment is a direct invitation for his presence.

Many youth have had sad experiences, both physically, mentally, and spiritually, because they have become involved in Satan's games. Gregg Weaver, now an active member of the Church, relates how as an inactive teenager he learned of the powerful influence of Satan.

"One evening, my cousin Susan, another girl and I decided to have some fun with a Ouija board while her parents were out for the evening. We were quite delighted to find that we could make it work — it would actually answer our questions! We were really 'grooving along,' having a great time asking it the kinds of questions you would think a thirteen-year-old would have on his mind: 'What am I going to be? Who will I marry?'

"We then began to ask questions of a little more serious nature:

" 'Would you lie to us?'

" 'Yes.'

" 'What is your purpose?'

" 'Evil.'

" 'Who is your enemy?'

" 'J. C.'

" 'Would you harm us?'

" 'Yes!'

"The mood and climate in the room had quickly changed from one of fun to a repressive, stifling atmosphere. It was now as if our minds were channeled into this dominating force — that we no longer had a choice or free agency. We felt trapped — unable to leave this engrossing evil and fearful as to what was to happen next — as we could feel the presence of Satan in the room.

"My cousin, Jimmy, an LDS priest, entered the room, and, needing little explanation of what had been going on, used his priesthood to command the evil spirits to depart. I didn't really understand what he was doing, but I did know that it worked, and that we were now free from that terrifying evil influence.

"I then knew without a doubt that there was a devil, that he really existed, and that he desired my personal destruction." (Gregg Weaver, "Cooperation with the Adversary," from *When Faith Writes the Story*, compiled by Margie Calhoun Jensen, Bookcraft, 1973, pages 207-208.)

The scriptures repeatedly warn us against becoming involved with spiritualistic matters. "There shall not be found among you any one that maketh his son or his daughter to pass through the fire, or that useth divination, or an observer of times, or an enchanter, or a witch,

"Or a charmer, or a consulter with familiar spirits, or a wizard, or a necromancer.

"For all that do these things are an abomination unto the Lord: and because of these abominations the Lord thy God doth drive them out from before thee." (Deuteronomy 18: 10-12.)

Divination refers to the art or practice of foreseeing or foretelling future events through the aid of supernatural powers. A necromancer is one who conjures up the spirits of the dead for purposes of magically revealing the future or influencing the course of events. These things are not in harmony with the gospel of Jesus Christ.

Satan is real. He does have power. Don't invite him into your life through any form of spiritualism. Should you find yourself in company where spiritualistic things are taking place, excuse yourself from the room. This is what the Lord expects from his covenant children, Saints in the church of Jesus Christ. The scriptures tell us: "Choose you this day whom ye will serve; . . .but as for me and my house, we will serve the Lord." (Joshua 24:15.) If you ardently desire to serve the Lord, Satan with his many techniques for destroying your soul will not be able to affect you.

Elder George A. Smith, a member of the Council of the Twelve in the days of the Prophet Joseph Smith, told an old Chinese fable about a man who was traveling through a strange country. In his travels he came upon a rich, beautiful and spacious city. As he viewed the city he commented to his guide, "The people in this city must be very righteous because I can only see one little devil in this entire large city."

The guide informed him that he was wrong. "This city is so perfectly given up to wickedness, corruption, degradation, and abomination of every kind, that it requires but one devil to keep them all in subjection."

Traveling on they saw a man climbing a rugged path. He was surrounded by seven huge, coarse-looking devils. "Why this must be a tremendously wicked man," the traveler asked. "See how many devils there are surrounding him."

Again the guide informed the traveler that he was wrong. "That man is the most righteous man in the country and those seven giant devils are constantly trying to turn him from his path, but they cannot."

Anyone who attempts to keep the commandments and live the principles of the gospel of Jesus Christ will also be subject to the close attention of Satan. He will do everything in his power to pull you off course. He will make the junk foods discussed in this chapter appear very appetizing. But don't partake. Keep your moral fiber strong and healthy and you will have the fortitude necessary to stick to your path, regardless of how rugged it may be, and no number of devils will be able to keep you from reaching your goal — exaltation.

7

The Cocreative Power

As we begin this chapter I want you to stretch your imagination. I want you to imagine that you are Satan.

In this imagined role you have observed the human scene for six thousand years or so — not as a passive observer, of course, but as an active worker against God and man. You are completely familiar in theory with the commandments of God; and since, as the scripture says, you are seeking to make all men miserable like yourself, during the life span of humanity on this earth you have been and still are anxiously engaged in promoting every kind of wickedness and vice. Because you have a tremendously high IQ your ingenuity is boundless. Accordingly you are continually improving upon the techniques of temptation you have developed over the centuries.

Naturally you learned long ago that the bigger the sin the more misery for the sinner. Consequently your interest in the smaller sins is principally that they are stepping-stones to greater ones. What really does the job is the big sin. Of course, you've learned to be tolerant. You'll work along with the slower learners, bringing them from a lower degree of sin to a higher one, in the hope that eventually they'll make the big leagues.

Murder is a good goal to aim at, since it is just about the

biggest sin you can bring anyone to. In terms of numbers you've had considerable success on this one. In America alone, thousands of people murder every year. It would be nice if you could dramatically improve upon the figures, and you are certainly doing your best. But as you review the situation you have to reluctantly admit that there are still far too many people in the world who have an unreasonable respect for human life, who just don't seem to have the right potential in this area. They simply aren't murder material.

Now, if you can't expect to make really significant advances on the murder front, where will you turn your attention? If you can't hinder God's purposes further by cutting off more and more human lives before their work on earth is done, at the same time propelling the murderers toward hell, what is the next best area to work in? What is the next greatest sin? The answer is immediately obvious to you — the sin of unchastity, sexual immorality.

In the temptation factor this sin has several advantages over murder. For example, everyone has a built-in sexual drive, bestowed by God himself for the purpose of procreating life. You can't know exactly what this urge feels like, of course, because you've never had a physical body; but your observation is that it's not too difficult to get most people to use that God-given urge for your purposes if you can just get them to move in your direction, if you can just get them to bring their rising emotional chemistry to the point which for most people, you've noticed, is the point of no return.

You've been pretty successful with this one tool over the centuries, and as you mentally review your past techniques you know why. Those techniques worked very well in their time. There were always those who would respond to the thought, "It's nice — it's fun." In earlier years particularly, though, a far greater proportion of people were ridiculously conscientious about the moral law, and for them you had to use a different approach. "It won't matter just this once," worked pretty well with some. So did "No one will know." More subtle still was your approach: "So what! You'll be beaten with a few stripes and then you'll be saved." A few thousand years of spreading the good word in such terms and you had hooked a lot of people. Then you came up with that beauty, "Everybody's doing it."

And about the same time as that one you coined the outstanding phrase, "There's no devil." No devil, no temptation, obviously no sin. Brilliant!

But things are speeding up now on all fronts. Everyday you're gaining more and more followers. Every day the battle line is more clearly drawn, as increasing numbers on your side and on the Lord's side stand up to be counted. Like the other areas, this segment of the battlefield must make its big push. There's still a great potential in this immorality weapon, but somehow the old battle-cries, the lies of the past, are not bringing the vast numbers flocking to your banner that you need for the big latter-day attack. In the second half of the twentieth century, you need the one big lie which perhaps will sweep you to victory. What shall it be?

If you really were Satan pondering this theme, what do you suppose you would come up with? Well, it's certain you could not better the one he in fact *did* come up with. In his diabolical way it was the most brilliant of them all — the really BIG LIE. The big lie he has spread, and which has been accepted in the minds of millions today, is that the sex act is perfectly natural and therefore is never wrong. His logical follow-up on that concept is that everyone everywhere can now throw away all sexual restraint.

That conclusion is of course the exact opposite of the truth, for in this matter restraint is precisely the name of the game. The true principle is worlds above Satan's degrading concept. It is that the proper exercise of the sexual urge in marriage makes a man and woman creators of a physical body which will clothe a spirit fathered by God; that they thus become actually and literally cocreators with God himself; and that the divinely given process which has such magnificent consequences must be sustained as just that and not degraded to the position of a mere appetite to be appeased at whim. Anyone who trifles with this power, seeks to deflect it from its appointed course, cheapens it in any way, is greatly offending the God who gave it. And that same God has commanded that we properly control our sexual urge, and has characterized as unclean anyone who indulges in the sex act outside of marriage. He has also said that no unclean thing can enter his presence.

I bring you the preceding paragraph as a very brief summary of this theme, about which no doubt you have heard in more detail many times. Along with the other principles of the gospel, that tremendously important concept was well understood by Adam and by the other ancient patriarchs and prophets. They tried diligently to maintain these gospel principles in the minds and hearts of men, while at the same time Satan, working through any who would follow him, brought his opposing doctrines into the world to whatever extent he could get them accepted.

You are familiar with what we call the Great Apostasy, the falling away from the Christian faith which Jesus had personally established on the earth. There were previous eras of apostasy too, of man-made changes in true doctrines, ordinances and standards. This subject usually brings to mind such matters as men changing the baptismal ordinance from immersion to sprinkling, or teaching and believing that God is a formless spirit instead of the personal, physical Being that ancient and modern prophets declare him to be. Such changes are indeed marks of apostasy. But if we look a little closer we will see that the changed and still deteriorating concepts about man's cocreative power are likewise a part of the world's falling away from God's revealed truths. It is an ongoing apostasy, in fact, and presumably will continue so until Satan is bound.

In chapter 2 I mentioned the benevolent effect of God's laws, the fact that they are all made for our benefit and not for his personal pleasure or for purposes of being deliberately restrictive. We would expect, then, to be able to see in the law of chastity some definite basic benefit to man. If I were asked to name this benefit, or at least a major benefit, I believe I would say that it is peace of mind.

Now, I am well aware of the arguments for permissiveness and the "new morality" of the day — that the removal of sexual restraints eliminates tensions and hangups and therefore gives a new and relaxing feeling to life. This is all part of the big lie. It simply is not so. Oh, of course in the beginning people may be deluded into thinking this to be true, but the longer-term results always disillusion them. The fact is that there is no peace in life without stability, without a firm hold on some fundamental and eternal principles. Those who violate such a crucial and eternal principle as chastity are not at peace because they have cut loose from a major spiritual anchor.

If you want confirmation of this, look at some of the prominent people leading the field in the "new morality." Frequently we read of this or that movie personality who has at last found the "real thing," the love of his or her life. With rapturous expressions the two lovers appear before the camera and in press interviews declaring their delight in each other's love and company. They then go off to continue an immoral relationship which in fact they had already begun following or during the breakup of the previous immoral relationship each of them had had with someone else.

In its heyday that former liaison similarly was heralded with glistening eyes and expressions of delight as the one great love. Nothing is more certain than that the current relationship will come to an end like the last one when disillusionment sets in. And the situation is not too much different when the two persons go to the trouble of getting married, for the much-married celebrity with a string of divorces and five or six married partners in his or her past is surely not subscribing to the law of chastity.

Now, this kind of life obviously brings spells of short-term excitement, but between those short spells there is turmoil rather than stability and peace. And what of the not-too-distant future? Observe the newspaper reports and interviews on the current attitudes and feelings of some of those who were famous for "living it up" in this way ten or fifteen years ago, or longer. No longer young, frequently they find themselves alone. They staked everything on the excitement of the moment and it failed them, as it always must fail. They had never invested true love, and consequently had never found fulfillment in a loving unselfish relationship. Read between the lines and observe the sense of insecurity they live with and you will know what I mean when I say that unchastity drives away peace of mind.

There are two inescapable factors working against those who seek pleasure in immorality. First, they are trying to fight an eternal law, a law of God, and that's a war no one can win. Cecil B. DeMille put the result of that war in graphic terms once when he was talking about the Ten Commandments. He said, in substance: "No one can break the Ten Commandments. He can only break himself against them."

For centuries past, the law of chastity has been honored in civilized society, even though wicked people frequently have broken that law. Even in apostate Christianity, it has always been a fundamental principle, so strong was its emphasis in the original Christian doctrine, though regrettably some churches and individual ministers are diluting the acceptance of this principle today. The person brought up in a Christian country therefore has not only the innate objections of the divine spirit within him if he should seek to break this law; he has also centuries of inherited tradition in mortality which likewise protest against immorality, the "sexual revolution" of recent years notwithstanding.

The second factor we cannot escape is that everyone is born with the Light of Christ, and that Spirit will guide him to the extent that he will allow it to. Many people relate that Spirit to the conscience which each person has, the voice which protests internally when we commit wrongdoing. We may silence the voice of conscience temporarily by various devices, but always, sooner or later, it will catch up with us. The person who does not have peace with his conscience has no peace with anything worthwhile. Either in this life or the next he will have to make that peace, and the longer he waits the bigger the price he pays to make it. "We lose the peace of centuries," it has been truly said, "when we seek the rapture of moments."

You who read this book, of course, have taken upon yourselves the gospel covenants, which the world in general has not. Since where much is given much is expected, there certainly will be no peace of mind for a Latter-day Saint who is unchaste. "Self-indulgence tastes good," wrote Frank Crane, "but remember the price — self-loathing." If you think this an extreme statement, check with a bishop who has had experience in interviewing those who have fallen into sexual sin. I assure you that when the person comes to himself, casts away his rationalizations and recognizes the need to tread the path of repentance, that "rapture of moments" is long since buried beneath a heap of guilt, torment and self-accusation.

A stake president told me of an experience in which a young

woman, an ex-missionary, came to his office in tears. She poured out to him this story: At the suggestion of a friend, seeking a little "excitement," she accompanied the other girl into a bar. She hadn't intended to get into sin, but the environment she had voluntarily entered was all set up for it. A man came up and spoke to her. He offered to buy her a drink; and having gone as far as she had, she took the next "exciting" step and foolishly accepted. It was the only alcoholic drink she had ever had in her entire life, she told the president. Less than an hour later she was in a motel room with this total stranger, to whom she then surrendered her virtue.

Now, in the stake president's office, she was in mental and spiritual agony. "Why did I do it?" she moaned. "How could I have done such an awful thing, when I knew it to be horribly wrong? President, I feel so ashamed and unclean." It would take a lot of godly sorrowing and anguished repenting before that young woman would feel that God had forgiven her and she could again enjoy peace of mind.

Nor is the offender the only one whose peace of mind is affected in such circumstances. In the Church we sometimes think that, since we have our free agency, we can choose to do whatever we feel like doing, and that if it's wrong we are only hurting ourselves. That is another of Satan's old lies. There is not a shadow of truth in it. Do you think the parents and other loved ones of the young woman I have just mentioned could have been unaffected by her transgression? Obviously her act and its results would have hurt them deeply. So if you transgress, chalk one up against yourself because you knew better. Chalk one up against your mother and father. Chalk one up against your bishop and your stake president, because if you fail, in a measure they also fail. The Lord has given all these people a stewardship over you, and there is no way for them not to be involved in your life.

Having suffered and triumphed over the worldly temptations himself, and being the Author of salvation to us all, the Lord well understands sin and its effects. His offer to us is the peace that the gospel brings. The commandment of chastity, like all his other commandments, is indeed given for our benefit. "Sin is not hurtful because it is forbidden," said Benjamin Franklin, "but it is forbidden because it is hurtful." Self-control is and always will be inseparable from peace of mind. Even the decent non-Christian recognizes this. Plato wrote: "The first and best victory is to conquer self. To be conquered by self is of all things the most shameful and vile."

One might wonder, since unchastity is such a great sin, why any members of the Church fall for the temptation. There may be several possible answers to that question. Some Church members are not strong enough in the faith to recognize the deep significance of all its principles and to live by them. Some get caught up in the follies and rationalizations and wickedness of the modern world and for a while try to convince themselves that there is no harm in the act. Others, like the girl in the bar, deliberately or inadvertently get themselves into circumstances where the temptation is intensified, and they eventually succumb.

There may be a perverse kind of satisfaction in sin at the time it is committed, but Alma's words nevertheless ring through the ages — "wickedness never was happiness." (Alma 41:10.) Satan knows this very well but he too often manages to convince people to the contrary, at least long enough for them to commit the sin. And, of course, the punishment is usually delayed — it is a case of "sin now, pay later." But for this delay factor, Satan would have a hard time tempting us. The particular sin we are discussing offers him another great advantage — the normal human being's divinely given physical urge can lean toward it if allowed to get out of hand.

There are of course those who somehow feel that they are missing something by not having the "fun" which the big world offers. I knew a young lady, whose parents joined the Church when she was two or three years old, who somehow couldn't settle down and in her late teens decided that she must see what the world had to offer. To the sorrow of her parents she left home and her hometown to try to get this out of her system. The parents were distressed by what this lovely girl was doing — the nightlife, the parties, the smoking and drinking she had now taken up, at least as social openers — but they could do nothing about it. Think of the tremendous risks this girl took by her urge to "live it up," to somehow cram all of life's experiences into her own life.

We not only cannot get all of life's experiences into one life, but, insofar as those experiences are unwholesome or potentially so, we shouldn't even try. It is altogether too dangerous to get even close to them. I am reminded of the story about the president of the ocean liner company who decided he would take a voyage on one of his ships. As the vessel was making its way away from port it had to journey near dangerous channels. He thought he would go and talk to the pilot. He found him to be an older man, agile and alert.

As he stood by the man at the wheel and engaged him in conversation, the president asked him questions about his occupation. One of the questions was, "I suppose you know all the dangerous places in this channel."

"No," was the terse reply.

"You don't! Then why on earth are you in charge of that wheel?"

"I know where the dangerous places *aren't*."

You might take a tip from this pilot. You don't have to know where the dangerous places are so much as where they are not, so that you can travel in those safe channels. There are many experiences in life that you don't need, either because they are in the dangerous channels or so close to them that you could easily fall in. Don't ever be tempted to "live it up" in the worldly sense.

I wish I could tell you that yours is the only age group that faces the problem of unchastity. It is not so. Unfortunately older people in the Church sometimes fall into this trap. Bear in mind that the sex act outside of the marriage relationship is always wrong. You have many bad examples in society at large, and now and again you will find one even in the Church. You will hear that so-and-so has been excommunicated or disfellowshipped, and perhaps it will come to your ears that the reason is the sin of unchastity, the violation of the marriage vow. But whoever falls, that is no excuse for you to fall. The Lord has not said he will compare you or me with some other human being, good, bad or indifferent. Rather, he will compare our efforts with the higher goal — in a sense, ultimately with himself. "Be ye therefore perfect, even as your Father which is in heaven is perfect," the Savior said.

With such a celestial goal in view no true Latter-day Saint wants to be crawling in the mud of a telestial sin like unchastity.

Of course, as we have seen, it is all a part of Satan's technique to have you believe that immorality is not really a serious sin — for him, that is the next best thing to your believing that it is not a sin at all. He has succeeded in convincing a tremendous proportion of God's children, but you must not be misled in this way.

The prophet Alma put this sin at its correct calibration point in the scale of iniquity — right next to murder. His son Corianton had been guilty of it, and as a loving father Alma was striving to bring him to repentance. Here is what he said about the sin itself: "Know ye not, my son, that these things are an abomination in the sight of the Lord; yea, most abominable above all sins save it be the shedding of innocent blood or denying the Holy Ghost?" (Alma 39:5.)

Notice Alma's use of the words *abomination* and *abominable*. These words carry a dictionary definition connoting extreme disgust and hatred, even loathing. If you examine the scriptures you will find that the Lord and his prophets repeatedly use these expressions in reference to murder and to sexual sin. The book of Moses, for example, talks about abominations obtained from Cain, who was the first murderer. In referring to the notorious secret combinations, the Book of Mormon refers to murders and abominations. The prophet Jacob, in his forthright speech condemning some of the men of his time for their unfaithfulness to their wives, refers to their wickedness and abominations. From these and other similar references there is no doubt that in the eyes of the Lord, as of everyone who is aspiring someday to be like him, unchastity is deep sin.

Why does this sin of unchastity find itself next to murder on the list? Perhaps because, while murder cuts off a life, unchastity tampers with and pollutes the springs and sources of life. Hear the pleading of President David O. McKay:

" . . . Your virtue is worth more than your life. Please, young folk, preserve your virtue even if you lose your lives. Do not tamper with sin . . . do not permit yourselves to be led into temptation. Conduct yourselves seemly and with due regard, particularly you young boys, to the sanctity of womanhood. Do not pollute it."

With all these warnings ringing in your ears and with the temptations to this sin constantly around you, how are you going to stay clear of it? Would you think me strange if I said you should even be afraid of it? I believe that a person should have such a healthy fear of this sin, as of something that the Lord does indeed abominate (as distinct, of course, from abominating the sinner), that he could never bring himself to do it.

So that such a fear will not be overcome by the stronger if softer emotions of the moment, you will be well advised not to get even near to the point of committing the act. I talked earlier of Satan's knowledge about the "point of no return." If you don't approach *that* point you won't slip over the edge. Notice what the Lord says: "Thou shalt not steal; neither commit adultery, nor kill, nor do anything like unto it." Homosexual activity is something "like unto it." Petting is something "like unto it," and will rapidly lead to the real thing. Elder Boyd K. Packer gave an outstanding address on this subject at April conference, 1972. After discussing some of Satan's techniques as manifest in the modern world and cautioning youth not to pervert and misuse the sacred power within them, he went on: "Do not let anyone at all touch or handle your body, not anyone! Those who tell you otherwise proselyte you to share their guilt. We teach you to maintain your innocence."

Part of the solution is not to linger with the thought. Every sin, especially every premeditated sin, is a thought before it becomes an action. Eliminate the unworthy action by cutting off the unworthy thought, which in turn means substituting a good and uplifting thought for the bad one. The person who encourages the unwholesome thought to linger with him is making it welcome; it will certainly return again and again, all the while seeking to carry out its work of bringing about the decision to act.

Don't be afraid to run from this sin — I mean literally run. Your great ancestor Joseph set you the proper example in this respect. At a large gathering of youth I heard President Spencer W. Kimball speak on this theme. He recounted how Joseph, who had been sold into Egypt by his brothers as a slave, was made overseer over the house of Potiphar. He talked about Potiphar's wife. She was sexy. She had perfumes that would give off a sweet fragrance. She had the finest clothes, gauzes and linens that money could buy. She had jewels to adorn her body. She was not homely; she was a beautiful woman. And as Joseph went back and forth carrying out his duties, she began to lust after this fine, clean, virile young man. Her lust grew until it consumed her. Finally she approached him and said, "Joseph, come and lie with me."

Joseph did not need to ponder this request, for had he not made the decision earlier by conforming his life to the highest moral standards? His reply gave the youth of all generations the formula for resisting sexual temptation: "How can I do this great wickedness, and sin against God?"

Potiphar's wife would not take no for an answer but day by day persisted with her enticing words and deeds. Even though in her position she had power to do him much harm, Joseph still refused. One day she managed to get close to him, began to embrace him; but he slipped away and fled from her and from the temptation that she represented. He was still not allowing the thought to linger in his mind. When temptations come to you in this area, as they very well may do, take strength from Joseph and say in your heart, "How can I do this great wickedness and sin against God?" Then get away fast. Running from sin is not cowardice but good common sense.

Hundreds of years after Joseph's experience another great man was faced with a similar though not as pressing a temptation. When the Lord selected this man to be the king of Israel, he described him as "a man after mine own heart," and David went on to become a great man and a great king. But one day he saw from a distance a beautiful woman, and when he inquired he found that she was someone else's wife. Instead of fleeing from the temptation as Joseph had done, he allowed his mind to linger on the thought and as a result in due course committed the act. To cover that act he later committed murder. David's losses for his "moment of rapture" are incredibly vast. Everybody loses who is involved in sexual transgression — everyone except Satan, that is.

Without going over exactly the same ground as may have been covered for you on other occasions, I have tried in this chapter to bring to your attention the importance of chastity as one of the building blocks in the destiny you are creating for yourself. I have therefore emphasized the gravity of the sin of unchastity, the tampering with the sacred powers of cocreation.

I hope you are convinced that at all costs you must hold in deepest respect those powers within you and stay well away from the great sin.

But there will here and there be one who has already committed this sin or something "like unto it." If you are such a person, what is your position now?

It is not my purpose here to dwell at length upon this point, but I would not want to leave the impression that your situation in this case would be hopeless. Far from it. God is ever merciful to those who come to him and repent of their sins, and this sin can be repented of. Because it is so grave a sin it is more difficult to repent of than, shall we say, breaking the Word of Wisdom might be. But the way is provided. It can only be done, however, through proper confession to your bishop, who is the common judge in Israel and whose calling requires him to deal with this kind of situation and guide the offender to the point where he receives forgiveness from the Church. At the same time he can show you how to receive forgiveness from the Lord.

So if you have been involved in moral transgression in any respect, know that you cannot obtain peace and forgiveness in any other way. Do not delay, but begin right now to find that forgiveness and peace which is available through the gospel of Jesus Christ. And it will help you in the process if you will read that outstanding book by President Spencer W. Kimball, *The Miracle of Forgiveness.*

It occurs to me that perhaps some of the youth of the Church feel that this subject of chastity is being overworked in talks and presentations by Church leaders. We know, however, that with the world increasing in wickedness this is a temptation that will not go away. Satan will work ever harder to entice both the youth and older people into his web of sin; and, as I indicated earlier, he has a lot going for him in this particular area of wickedness. It follows that those in Church leadership positions who seek to combat him will be under the necessity of constantly raising their voices in warning and encouragement to the members of the Church.

This trend was most noticeable in the Swedish Area Conference which I attended in 1974, in which a special conference was held with the youth of the Scandinavian countries. In that conference President Kimball first called on Elder Ezra Taft Benson,

President of the Council of the Twelve Apostles, to speak. I was the second speaker and was followed by Elder Boyd K. Packer of the Council of the Twelve. President Kimball himself was the fourth speaker. All four speakers spoke on the same subject — sexual morality. The Lord did not want the LDS youth of those countries to be merely patted gently on the wrist about moral conditions surrounding them. Rather he hit them with such great impact that they could not misunderstand the situation. That forthright, unmistakable note of warning and encouragement is bound to continue as a counter to the increasing immorality of the world.

To sound that note is an inescapable responsibility of Church leaders both general and local. In concluding this chapter I cannot do better than bring you the words of President Stephen L Richards of the First Presidency, in which he told of a stake president's powerful presentation on this theme:

"Some years ago I presided over a stake conference session in one of our older meetinghouses in which there was a relatively small balcony in the rear of the chapel. The balcony was filled with young men and women in their teens. I called upon the president of the stake to speak at the conference. To my surprise, and I think to the surprise of the large congregation in the body of the house, he addressed himself directly and exclusively to the young people in the gallery. Looking straight at them, he said, in substance:

" 'Young people, in the not too distant future nearly every one of you will come to me to be interviewed: some for advancement in the priesthood — these will be young men; some for recommendations to go on missions — these will be both young men and young women; and many of you for recommendations to go to the temple for marriage — both young men and young women. When you come to me for interview separately, I will ask each one to sit down in a chair directly facing me. I will look each one squarely in the eye, and this is the first question I will ask: Are you clean? If you answer yes, you will be happy. If you answer no, you will be sorry. If you lie to me, you will regret it all the days of your life.'

"That is all that he said to these young people. There was profound silence. I think that no one who was present will ever forget the occasion and the impression made on these young men and women. I think that this man did not overemphasize the moral principle which he impressed on these young people. May it not be that when we come to the final judgment, as all of us will, that may be the first question propounded for each of us: Are you clean?"

8

Love Is a
Shining Thing

Have you ever wanted to do something really crazy? I guess everyone does now and then. I have a friend who, ever since he first learned about the continental divide, has had the crazy desire to stand on top of the highest peak of the divide with a huge bucket of water in hand. He would like to dump the water right on the very peak of the divide and watch half of it start its course to the Atlantic Ocean, the other half begin its trek to the Pacific. In reality, of course, my friend could never find such a definitive point, but the idea still fascinates him. He thinks it would be terribly exciting to actually follow a single drop of rain falling on top of the divide as it first forms a tiny rivulet, then a little brook, and next a stream. The stream would join with other streams to become a major tributary, eventually a mighty river, and finally part of a great ocean.

While we cannot watch a single drop of rain along each step of its course to the sea, you are at the age where very soon you will be able to watch something in your life grow from a tiny rivulet to a mighty, moving force. That something is love.

Many years ago a friend of mine shared with me a beautiful story about love entitled "Love Is a Shining Thing." I do not know who the author was, but I would like to share it with you.

"They sat together on the porch steps, so close that their moon shadow was a single wedge of blackness against the weathered wood. Tomorrow was the wedding, with all the excitement and confusion, tears and laughter. There would be no privacy then. But this quiet hour was their own.

"She said, 'It's peaceful, isn't it?' She was watching the great stately clouds march over their heads and drop from sight into the quick-silver sea. He was watching her, and thought that he had never seen her so beautiful.

"The wind blew; the waves made little hush, hush, sounds, sighing against the sand. 'You know,' she said, 'I always wondered how I'd feel the night before my wedding — scared, or thrilled, or uncertain, or what.'

" 'You're not scared, are you?'

" 'Oh, no,' she said quickly. She hugged his arm and put her face against his shoulder in the impulsive way she had. 'Just a little solemn, maybe. Solemn and gay, and young and old, and happy and sad. Do you know what I mean?'

" 'Yes,' he said, 'I know.'

" 'It's love that does it, I suppose,' she said. 'That old thing; we've never talked about it much, have we? About love itself, I mean.'

"He smiled a little. 'We never had to.'

" 'I'd sort of like to — now,' she said. 'Do you mind? I'd like to try to tell you how I feel, before tomorrow happens.

" 'Will it be any different after tomorrow?'

" 'No, but I may not be able to talk about it then. It may go somewhere deep inside, below the talking level.'

" 'All right,' he said, 'tell me about love.'

"She watched a cloud ravel itself against the moon. 'Well,' she said, 'to me it's a shining thing, like a golden fire or a silver mist. It comes very quietly, you can't command it, but you can't deny it either. When it does come, you can't see it or touch it, but you can feel it — inside of you and around you and around the person you love. It changes you; it changes everything. Colors are brighter, music sweeter, full little honeysuckles are heavenly food, funny things are funnier. Ordinary speech won't do — you grope for better ways to express how you feel. You read poetry. Maybe you even try to write it.'

"She leaned back, clasping her hands around her knees, the moonlight bright and ecstatic on her face.

" 'Oh, it's so many things! Waiting in the dark, waiting for the phone to ring, opening a box of flowers. It's holding hands in a movie; it's humming a sad little tune; it's walking in the rain; it's riding in a convertible with the wind in your hair; it's quarreling and making up again. It's that first warm drowsy thought in the morning and the last kiss at night. . . .'

"She broke off and suddenly gave him a desolate look. 'But it's all been said before, hasn't it?'

" 'Even if it has,' he told her gently, 'that doesn't make it any less true.'

" 'Maybe I'm just being silly,' she said doubtfully. 'Is that the way love seems to you?'

"He did not answer for a while. At last he said, 'I might add a little to your definition.'

" 'You mean you wouldn't change it?'

" 'No, just add to it.'

"She put her chin in her hands. 'Go ahead. I'm listening.'

"He took out the pen she had given him and looked at it for a long moment. 'You said it was a lot of little things. You're right. I could mention a few that don't have much glitter. But they have an importance that grows. . . .'

"She watched his lean fingers begin to move. 'Tell me,' she said.

" 'Oh, coming home to somebody when the day is ended — or waiting for somebody to come home to you. Giving or getting a word of praise when none is really deserved. Sharing a joke that nobody else understands. Planting a tree together and watching it grow. Sitting up with a sick child. Remembering anniversaries. Do I make it sound terribly dull?'

"She did not say anything; she shook her head.

" 'Everything you mentioned is a part of it,' he went on, 'but it's not all triumphant, you know. It's also sharing disappointment and sorrow. It's going out to slay the dragon, and finding the dragon too much for you, and running away — but going out again the next day. It's the little chips of tolerance that you finally knock off the granite of your own ego; not saying "I told you so," not noticing the dented fender on the family car. It's the ambitions you had for yourself, and planting them in your children. . . .' His voice trailed off into the glistening night.

" 'Are you talking,' she asked finally, 'about loving, or living?'

" 'You'll find,' he said, 'there's not much of one without the other.'

" 'When — when did you learn that?'

" 'Quite a while ago, before your mother died.' His hand touched her shining hair. 'Better get to bed now, baby. Tomorrow is your big day.'

"She clung to him suddenly. 'Oh, Daddy, I'm going to miss you so!'

" 'Nonsense,' he said. 'I'll be seeing you all the time. Run along now.'

"But after she was gone he sat there for a long time, alone in the moonlight."

Both the soon-to-be bride and her father were discussing the same subject — love. But to the young bride, love was still a small stream high up on the mountain. To her father, love had grown into a mighty river, deep and meaningful.

Within the next few years you will figuratively find yourself standing in a rain shower on top of the continental divide. But you will find that many drops of rain will disappear in thirsty ground or evaporate before they ever form that first tiny rivulet. That is because love has many counterfeits, and only the real thing will grow and deepen into a mighty river.

One of the most frequent counterfeits for love is physical attraction. While physical attraction is a vital and necessary part of a marriage relationship, it is only a manifestation of love and should not be mistaken for love. Someone once said, "A kiss is something that brings two people so close together that they cannot see anything wrong with each other." This is sad but sometimes true. When you are young, holding hands and kissing good night are new and exciting experiences and easily confused with love. But it is love, not just kissing, which brings people so close that they can overlook the faults in each other. In time you will learn to differentiate between just an arousing physical experience and a deeper emotional experience.

Infatuation is often mistaken for love. Infatuation is foolish or extravagant love or admiration. A girl may be infatuated with a fellow because he owns his own car, because he is on the football team, or because he takes her to nice places on a date. A fellow may be infatuated with a girl because she is affectionate, because she is a cheerleader, or because she is on the honor roll. This is foolish love, foolish admiration. It is easy to identify when you are on the outside looking in, but when you are the person involved it is more difficult to differentiate between love and infatuation. To help you make the distinction, ask yourself whether that person has that "certain something" or "something certain." If your answer is the former, chances are you are just infatuated.

Another common myth to be dispelled is the idea of "love at first sight." Love is like baking bread. Just because the necessary ingredients are present, love is not the spontaneous result. The relationship needs careful measuring, sifting, mixing and kneading. A lengthy time for proofing or raising is required before it undergoes the final and most demanding test — the hot oven. Real and lasting love is a developing relationship, not an abrupt awakening, and it must be tested by friendship, experience, adversity, and time.

Some young people confuse a need for security with love. This most frequently occurs in families where there is insufficient parental love. Often attention from a member of the opposite sex will bridge that gap — it is satisfying and need-fulfilling. Nearly everyone eventually wants a little place of their own, a steady job, a regular income, a family, a secure niche in society, but don't confuse an opportunity to satisfy this security need with love. Too many marriages which have been based on this need have ended in divorce, leaving the parties involved even more insecure.

Experiencing these many counterfeits is part of growing up. You don't need to feel embarrassed if someone accuses you of having a "puppy love" or an infatuation for someone. This is a normal experience. The desire for the security of a home and family of your own is also natural. And the need for physical affection is part of a God-given instinct. The important thing is to recognize these feelings for what they are and to not mistake them for love.

If you are of the appropriate age, date a wide variety of people. Then in time and with maturity you will begin to rec-

ognize the qualities which will contribute to an enduring relationship. Look for similarities in personal habits, character,
ambition, and outlook. Compare notes on educational background, social and economic standing, families, and religious
convictions. Listen to your head and not your heart. Remember
that makeup will wash off, hair styles will change, and clothing
will wear out — artificial attractions soon disappear. Is there
enough honest respect and admiration present to form that first
rivulet of love?

President Spencer W. Kimball made plain the distinction
between counterfeit love and mature love with these state-
ments:

"What is love? Many people think of it as mere physical
attraction and they casually speak of 'falling in love' and 'love at
first sight.' This may be Hollywood's version and the interpretation of those who write love songs and love fiction.

"True love is not wrapped in such flimsy material. One
might become immediately attracted to another individual, but
love is far more than physical attraction. It is deep, inclusive,
and comprehensive. Physical attraction is only one of the many
elements, but there must be faith and confidence and understanding and partnership. There must be common ideals and
standards. There must be a great devotion and companionship.

"Love is cleanliness and progress and sacrifice and selfless-
ness. This kind of love never tires nor wanes, but lives through
sickness and sorrow, poverty and privation, accomplishment
and disappointment, time and eternity.

"For the love to continue, there must be an increase constantly of confidence and understanding, of frequent and sincere expression of appreciation and affection. There must be a
forgetting of self and a constant concern for each other. Interests, hopes, objectives must be constantly focused into a single
channel."

A stream that is not fed by other streams will eventually dry
up and disappear. This too is true of love. Love is nurtured
through unselfish service to one another, "sacrifice and selfless-
ness," as President Kimball put it. Love has always been a
byproduct of service. Service to others, whether in the Church,
in the community, or at home, will cause love to grow.

At first love will be as the young bride described it —

"walking in the rain, riding in a convertible with the wind in your hair, quarreling and making up again" — a myriad of special experiences shared together. These are a beautiful part of falling in love. But as the stream merges with other streams and love matures, the glowing, palpitating, dazzling excitement of just being together will diminish and instead be replaced by a deep and genuine concern for the happiness of the other person. Individual and selfish needs will be forgotten in the presence of true love.

Dr. Abraham Stone, a marriage counselor, once said: "Mature love differs from childish love in that it desires not merely the satisfaction of self, of one's own needs, but even more the satisfactions of the mate. A couple maturely in love, genuinely 'care' for one another. They want to establish a kinship of body and feeling. They do not romantically endow each other with illusionary qualities, but see and accept in one another both virtues and faults."

Shakespeare went one step further in describing love. He said, "Thou blind fool, love, what dost thou to mine eyes,/That they behold and see not what they see." This "blindness" is both a blessing and a curse. It is a curse to those who are merely infatuated, preventing them from objectively viewing another person. But to those maturely in love, that blindness is a blessing; it should make us blind only to another's follies. It should enable us to magnify virtues and minimize faults.

Mature love also has the ability to endure trials and testing. As the wise father in the story said   t all triumphant." Adversity will come to every home, whether it be economic setback, loss of health, death of a loved one, or some other form of difficulty. But mature couples who genuinely love each other will together face disappointment and sorrow, and their love will grow as a result of it.

Many years ago I was in another city for stake conference and a woman I had previously known asked if I would give her a blessing. I agreed and we arranged to meet following the leadership meeting on Saturday night. She arrived with her bishop and his wife, a counselor in her bishopric and his wife, and another couple who were close friends. When I saw her I immediately asked, "Sister _____ , where is your husband?"

"Brother Featherstone," she began, "that is part of my problem. A few months ago the doctors discovered that I have cancer and they have given me only a few months to live. As soon as my husband heard this news he left. He has abandoned me and our three children. I don't know where he is; we haven't heard from him in several months. I am going to be operated on on Tuesday, and I would like a special blessing, not for me, but for my children. You see, my children have no relatives, no one to raise them except my husband, and we don't know where he is. Would you ask God to permit me to live long enough to raise my three little babies. If he would let me do that, then he could take me any time."

I was filled with absolute compassion for this sister. As I listened to her story I thought, "If I were the God of heaven I believe I would heal her." We knelt together. The bishop anointed the sister's head, and I sealed the anointing. Then we parted. I conducted the following sessions of conference and traveled back to Salt Lake City the next day.

The following Tuesday night I received a phone call from the lovely couple who had been with Sister _____ when she received her blessing. They said: "When the doctors operated on Sister _____ they said that truly a notable miracle had been done. They were able to solve the problem and from all appearances Sister _____ will live a long life and be able to raise her children."

I wept as I heard these words, grateful that the Lord had granted a blessing to this faithful woman whose absolute love for her children exceeded any thought of self or concern for her own welfare.

This story dramatically illustrates the difference between mature and immature love. The wife knew the meaning of unselfish, Christlike love. Her husband was selfish beyond expression, unable to face life and make the necessary adjustments to the sometimes terrible, sometimes staggering problems which life may deal out.

Thomas Carlyle said, "The brightest crowns that are worn in heaven have been tried and smelted and polished and glorified through the furnace of tribulation." And this is never more true than in love and marriage.

As the wise father concluded, love is "going out to slay the dragon, and finding the dragon too much for you, and running away — but going out again the next day. It's the little chips of tolerance that you finally knock off the granite of your own ego; not saying 'I told you so,' not noticing the dented fender on the family car. It's the ambitions you had for yourself, and planting them in your children. . . ." Love is life. "There's not much of one without the other." Love is practical and realistic, yet it is so powerful that it can be the most moving force in the world. The French scientist de Chardin said: "Someday, after we have mastered the winds, the waves, the tides, and gravity, we will harness for God the energies of love: And then, for the second time in the history of the world, . . . man will have discovered fire!"

As de Chardin suggested, love has a great power to motivate. That is why mature love can be compared with the mighty Mississippi River. But remember that even the waters of the Mississippi started as tiny rivulets high up on the continental divide. May you be blessed as you discover the first rivulets of love. May you have success as you seek your eternal mate and begin to put into motion that great river, that shining thing — love.

9

Looking
at Life

Fire once ripped through the library of Ralph Waldo Emerson, the famed American essayist and poet. As he stood and watched his most valued possessions go up in flames, Louisa May Alcott, a close friend of Emerson, expressed her sympathy for his loss.

"Never mind, Louisa," the man answered cheerfully. "See what a beautiful blaze they make!"

Wow! What a terrific attitude! What a magnificent way to look at life!

What kind of an attitude do you have toward life? One of the most valuable building tools you can acquire is a positive mental attitude. The ability to look at life cheerfully and optimistically can have a profound affect on every facet of your life — from your grade in American history to your 2½-minute talk in Sunday School; from your relationship with your "bratty" little brother to your popularity with the opposite sex. Let's look at some of the reasons why a positive attitude can make such a profound difference in our lives.

As illustrated by the story of Ralph Waldo Emerson, a positive attitude can help us accept adversity and turn disadvantages to advantages. I once heard of a woman who won first prize at a garden show for her exquisite white African violet.

The second-place winner questioned the judges' decision: "She couldn't have possibly grown that beautiful violet. She lives in an attic apartment without any light."

"That is not true," answered the blue-ribbon winner. "A small amount of light enters my apartment each day. I simply move my plant around to take advantage of the sunshine."

This woman knew how to turn a disadvantage to an advantage. She refused to be defeated by adversity. When life deals you a bad blow, how do you handle it?

Life dealt a bad blow to Tom Osmond, the oldest of the famed Osmond brothers. He was born deaf. As his younger brothers grew in popularity, Tom began to wonder why he had been given that particular infirmity. Why couldn't he be famous like his other brothers? He went to the scriptures in search of an answer and read:

"And as Jesus passed by, he saw a man which was blind from his birth. And his disciples asked him, saying, Master, who did sin, this man, or his parents, that he was born blind? Jesus answered, Neither hath this man sinned, nor his parents: but that the works of God should be made manifest in him." (John 9:1-3.)

"That's when it finally came to me," said Tom. "I was an individual. I had God-given talents. And even though I couldn't be a singer like the rest of my family, I still had something major to contribute with my life. I realized I had to stop pouting over my weaknesses. I needed to discover those talents, develop them, and use them to achieve my own success."

And that is exactly what Tom did. Although many people deemed it impossible, Tom taught himself to play the piano, the drums, and the saxophone. He learned to tap dance. And he mastered the skills of printing and photography, which now provide his livelihood. (From "Our Family Motto," by Chris and Tom Osmond, *The New Era*, April 1977.)

Tom learned that the difference between a stumbling block and a stepping stone is often just a matter of attitude.

How do you handle problems and adversities? If you're a girl and you seldom or never date, do you sit in front of the TV eating pizza and ice cream and lamenting your woes? Or are you busy learning new skills, acquiring new talents, and making yourself a more attractive and more dateable person? If you're a boy who just can't quite make the varsity football or basketball team, do you call yourself a failure and give up? Or do you decide that there are other areas in which you can "make the cut," such as running for a studentbody office, trying out for yell leader, taking a part in the school play, or just being the best waterboy the team has ever known?

Don't turn and run from adversity. Develop a positive attitude which enables you to make the best of disadvantages. A pearl, one of the most admired of all jewels, is a product of adversity. It is formed when a foreign object, such as a grain of sand, finds its way into the mother-of-pearl of a living oyster. This foreign particle causes the oyster great discomfort. To counteract the difficulty, the oyster forms a substance around the irritating object and a pearl is created.

The person who develops a proper attitude will find that every disadvantage can be made into a beautiful pearl.

Our attitude is critical to success. I would like to tell you about a friend of mine named Neal Schmidt and how his attitude helped him to succeed.

Neal and I grew up in the same ward. Neal was a few years younger than I. He was an exceptional athlete, especially good at pole vaulting. One summer Neal was employed at the same grocery store at which I worked. I decided one day that I would mark on the wall in the produce backroom a red line indicating how high Neal would have to pole vault to break the state record by six inches. By the red line I hung a sign which read: "Neal Schmidt will pole vault this high this coming track season and break the state record."

When Neal first saw the red line he thought that a jump of that height was impossible. But day after day as he looked at the line he wrapped his mind around the thought of breaking the state record by pole-vaulting the height of that line. Day after day he studied the red line, he practiced, and gradually his attitude changed. No longer did the height seem insurmountable. When the track meet finally came, Neal pole-vaulted over the height of the red line and broke the state record.

Attitude is critical to success. We need to learn to bury our old negative attitudes which say "I can't" and develop positive new attitudes which say "I can." William James, an American psychologist and philosopher, once said, "That which holds the attention determines the action." In other words, where the mind goes the feet will surely follow. If we make up our mind that we can succeed, we will.

Tom Osmond said of success: "In my struggles I have learned that there are more than just physical handicaps. There are handicaps of attitudes also that hold back far more people from success than the physical kind. Many individuals believe they can never achieve success, so they never try. Some even preprogram themselves to fail before they ever start."

Do you remember the story of the little train chugging up the steep hill? Each turn of the wheels seemed to say "I think I can, I think I can, I think I can." And he did succeed.

Attitude will also determine in large measure the type of person *you* will be. Elder Marvin J. Ashton tells of a man he met who had tattooed on his body the words "BORN LOSER." You probably won't be surprised to learn that Elder Ashton met this man in prison.

Contrast the attitude of the prison inmate with that of a young man named Stephen Farrance. When Stephen was four years old it was discovered that he had a muscle disease which, if it progressed, would take his life by the time he was twelve. And unfortunately the disease did progress. First Stephen's tendons pulled his feet up so that he had to walk on his toes. Then his neck muscles degenerated and could no longer support his head; his head flopped back. Finally the disease progressed to the stage that his distorted body was almost doubled over and he spent most of his time, awake or asleep, draped over a chair.

But as devastating as the disease was on Stephen's body, it did not affect his spirit. He had the attitude, "I'm not going to let *me* get me down." And he didn't.

He was the scorekeeper for the basketball team, manager of one of the girls' teams, on the staff of the school newspaper, and elected to various student-council offices. When he ran for treasurer he said in his campaign speech, "You have only to take one look at me to be sure I won't run off with the funds!"

Stephen took an active part in Church programs. He went to Primary, was active in Cub Scouts, and went on into Scouting. He advanced in the priesthood and passed the sacrament for as long as he was physically able. Then he assisted with its preparation. He attended seminary regularly at 5:30 A.M. every morning

for four years. And he was a staunch supporter of the missionary program, inviting the elders into his home as often as possible.

Stephen loved drama. He directed, became the sound-
effects manager, and dabbled in lighting. Writing and directing
his ward roadshow was his last big venture. His show won the
award for "Best All-Round Entertainment." But Stephen never
saw that winning performance; he had died earlier that day. The
news of his passing was withheld from the cast and the audience
until the conclusion of the roadshow performances. "How could
his family be here tonight?" someone in the audience asked.
And the reply came, "After living with Stephen, what else could
they do?"

Stephen had the blessing of a keen mind, a lively sense of
humor, and the ability to see problems for what they were. He
was not superhuman. He had ups and downs, likes and dis-
likes, just the same as all of us. But he possessed one attribute
which many of us as yet need to develop — a positive attitude:
"I'm not going to let *me* get me down." His attitude, not his
physical circumstances, determined what he made of himself.
"For as he [a man] thinketh in his heart, so is he." (Proverbs
23:7.) (From "Stephen," by Pene Horton, *The New Era*, May
1976.)

"The greatest discovery of my generation," said William
James, "is that you can change your circumstances by changing
your attitudes of mind." And how true that is! Charles E. Jones
in his book *Life Is Tremendous* tells of a young man who had come
to see him after graduating number two in his class from an Ivy
League college. This young man had had several job offers from
outstanding companies, but he could not get excited about accepting any of them. He felt that he would not like working for
any of the companies. Charles Jones answered the young man
with this powerful sermon on attitude:

"I've been learning that life is not doing what you like to do.
Real life is doing what you *ought* to do. I've been learning that
people who do what they like to do eventually discover that
what they thought they like to do they don't like to do, but
people who are learning to do what they don't like to do but
ought to do, eventually discover that what they thought they
didn't like to do they do like to do."

Most of us are happy or unhappy not because of our circumstances but because of what we think about our circumstances. The secret then is to change your attitude about those things which make you unhappy or about those things you don't particularly like. In time you will find that a change of attitude will change the circumstances. For example, perhaps you dislike school and your report card shows a less-than-satisfactory performance. Begin by telling yourself that you can get better grades. Develop the determination to do something about it. Then couple that determination with earnest study and hard work. You will be rewarded with better grades and a healthier attitude toward school.

Maybe you are dissatisfied with your summer employment or after-school job. Perhaps you don't like the work or wish that it was more interesting. Tell yourself that it is a fascinating job — then act like it. Try to learn as much as you can about the company. Consider your position to be the most vital job in the organization. Then constantly look for ways to do your job better, quicker, and more efficiently. In time and with sincere effort you too will discover that what you didn't like to do you do like to do.

Perhaps a look in the mirror reveals a face, figure or physique not quite to your liking. Don't consider yourself a hopeless case. Decide that you can be more physically attractive, then go to work on it. Eat better, sleep more, get on a daily exercise program, see a dermatologist, restyle your hair, spruce up your wardrobe, or whatever. But first, change your attitude about yourself. Decide that you like yourself and that you *can* be a becoming person.

As you go about the do-it-yourself project of building you, don't be discouraged if every facet of you is not exactly as you would like it to be. Certainly change what you can, but then change your attitude about the rest. You will find that by changing your attitude your circumstances will eventually change.

As in all things the Savior gave us the best example of proper attitude. His life was beset with trials. He experienced hatred, ridicule and abuse. His hometown scorned his achievements. Some of his disciples turned away from him. His enemies bitterly persecuted him. And his own people cruelly crucified him. Yet his words and actions always evidenced his character, his conviction, courage and proper attitude. He did not complain or retaliate. He did not find fault. He did not admit defeat. Instead he said, "Let not your heart be troubled." (John 14:1.)

The Savior had a great mission to fulfill — a mission which would not permit an attitude of defeat. We too have an important mission to accomplish. There is a great work ahead for all of us. Life is a magnificent challenge and we must prepare to meet that challenge and fulfill our destiny by developing an unconquerable spirit and an attitude toward success. My young friends, learn now to look at life optimistically and positively. Then as you assemble each piece of your do-it-yourself destiny you will be rewarded with happiness, success, and true accomplishment.

10

Prepare
to Lead

Have you played the word-association game in which someone calls out a word and you say the first thing that comes to your mind? If I said "leader," what would be your first thought? Maybe you would think of the opposite — a follower. Maybe you would think of someone at school — a cheerleader, the quarterback on the football team, the principal. Or perhaps your father, your bishop, your priesthood quorum or class president would come to mind. But would you think of yourself? Do you consider yourself a leader?

Everyone can be a leader in some way. In some people, leadership qualities are readily apparent; in others, these traits need some developing. Every member of the Lord's church has opportunities to lead. The sweet quiet girl in Sunday School class who shows the others how to be reverent is a leader just as much as the rebel who's trying to lead the class astray. But regardless of where you fall on the leadership scale — from an obedient follower to an enthusiastic leader — now is the time to begin to improve your leadership abilities and to make leadership an important part of your do-it-yourself destiny.

Once you realize that you already are a leader in some way, it's easier to begin to improve your leadership potential. Don't be afraid of leadership. Yes, it takes a lot more courage to be out in front than to be just lost in the crowd. But realize that everyone who assumes a leadership position at times feels inadequate and frightened.

I was most impressed by some thoughts Charlton Heston expressed about the prophet Moses whom he portrayed in the movie *The Ten Commandments.* The actor had always envisioned Moses as a stern, God-like figure with a long white beard. But as he studied the character of the prophet while filming the movie, he suddenly saw Moses as a man of flesh and blood. He saw him struggling up the cliffs of Mount Sinai, sandals torn, hair blown by the desert wind, heart pounding, eyes wide with fear and apprehension. He saw that the man who ascended that mountain toward the burning bush was just an ordinary man.

Second, he glimpsed Moses fleeing from the wrath of Pharoah. Moses had not yet received his divine commission. He was a man running for his life, fleeing Pharoah's death sentence, only to find a more hideous death threatening him under the pitiless sun. Where was Moses, the honored patriarch? Here only was an exhausted man, a man who, once at least, had hit rock bottom.

The third glimpse Charlton Heston had of Moses was as the prophet walked among the motley, sweating mass of Israelites which he was to lead out of captivity. Their clothes were ragged, their animals were skinny; only a waterless, unrelenting desert stretched ahead.

The Moses Charlton Heston had seen could not lead these people out of captivity, out into the desert — not the Moses that had crawled on his knees through that very desert, not the man who had struggled up Mount Sinai, panting and terrified. That man was capable of fear and doubt.

"Of course Moses could not lead these thousands across the desert," Charlton Heston concluded. "He never would have tried. But God could do it. And Moses, this all-too-human man, this man so much like the rest of us, had simply turned himself into the instrument through which the strength of God moved."

Was Moses really any different than you and I? Yes, he was a prophet of God, but he was, nevertheless, very much a man. And like every man who finds himself in a position of leadership, at one time or another he felt inadequate. He had doubts and fears about his ability to lead, but he went forth with courage and faith and the Lord made him equal to his calling.

The Lord will do the same for us. When we find ourselves in leadership positions in the Lord's kingdom we are given strength and an inner-well of confidence which blesses us and helps us reach pinnacles of achievement of which we had never before dreamed. Our responsibility is simply to commit ourselves to do the very best we possibly can and leave the rest for the Lord to accomplish through us.

This certainly doesn't mean that we can idly sit back, or indulge in low, demeaning behavior and still expect the Lord to help us. We must do everything we can to become good leaders, then we can expect the Lord to do the rest.

What qualities must we acquire if we want to be a modern-day Moses?

Before we can be effective leaders we must first be good followers. I once heard a story about a beautiful dapple-gray workhorse who was appropriately named Samson. Samson was an exhibitionist. When there was a load to be pulled he would prick up his ears and stamp his feet; he welcomed every opportunity to show his strength.

Samson always pulled in front of the other horses. When the keeper led him to the load and attached his chains to the shafts, Samson scarcely waited for the other horses. Head down, knees almost touching the ground, sparks flying from his hooves, he practically pulled the whole weight by himself.

Samson's keeper was frequently asked why he didn't give Samson a rest from his lead position. He replied that Samson wouldn't pull when back with the others because he couldn't show off there. He wouldn't cooperate unless he was in front, doing everything by himself.

One day a passerby noticed that Samson was not attached to the team at all. A strange horse was in his place. He inquired where Samson was and the keeper replied that Samson had died of overwork.

The story of Samson illustrates this very important principle of leadership: Leaders must also be good followers. But many leaders, however, are like Samson; they want all the work and glory for themselves and refuse to cooperate with others. The truly great leader is equally as willing to follow as he is to lead, just as willing to be directed as to direct.

In the Church there are many men and women who have held very responsible positions as bishops, stake and mission presidents, and Relief Society presidents, who are now happily serving as home and visiting teachers, Sunday School and Primary instructors. It is not the calling in which they serve which matters but the manner in which they serve. They are true leaders.

On the other hand, there are some who are envious of those in leadership positions and consequently do not have a sympathetic, charitable attitude toward their leaders. If they do not agree with someone in a position of authority over them, they speak ill of their leader and attempt to persuade others to their side. Another example of a poor follower is the person who does not respect those who are called to teach him. This person persists in questioning the advice of his teachers or in drawing the lesson off the subject in pursuit of his own gospel answers. People of that type don't possess the empathy or sensitivity necessary to be great leaders because they are not good followers. As you desire to become a great leader, first become a devoted, obedient follower.

Next, realize that leadership requires discipline. It is not happenstance that some people turn out to be leaders while others never amount to anything more than goof-offs. People who become leaders pay the disciplinary costs involved.

Not long ago I ran into a man with whom I had attended high school. In school this man was an A-1 goof-off. His report card showed a string of Cs, Ds, and incompletes. He was constantly being reprimanded for his "I-don't-care attitude" and his misbehavior. He barely graduated from high school. Today, however, he is an extremely successful sales executive. What made the difference? This man decided to discipline himself and to make something of his life. He decided to exercise the restraint, control and moderation necessary to achieve the end he sought. He decided to develop his leadership talents. If you want to be a leader, you must decide whether you are willing to pay the price by disciplining your life.

The discipline required depends on the particular field of

endeavor. For example, if you want to be an Olympic swimmer, before you can win a gold medal you must first discipline yourself to endure sometimes excruciating physical pain. Many years ago the coach of the Yale swim team was asked to what he contributed his great success in producing world-champion swimmers. He said he had learned how to discipline the swimmers to break the pain barrier. Regardless of the area in which you wish to lead, varying amounts of self-discipline will be required of you. You must submit yourself to a stricter personal discipline than is expected of others if you want to be a leader.

Vince Lombardi, the famed coach of the Green Bay Packers, made a profound statement in which he outlined another important quality of leadership: "One of the qualities of leadership which contributes most to success is seldom listed. The trait is often overlooked or unobserved because other factors stand out. It may be the reason for the drive or even the ambition. Certainly it contributes to the awareness and the constant emphasis for performance. It is the prime factor in the search for all information possible on which to make a decision. A leader constantly seeks ways to do whatever needs to be done better. If a person with this quality will continue positive application of this negative factor, that person will have a leadership role. The quality? *Dissatisfaction.*" Vince Lombardi believed that a leader was one who could make the unsatisfactory satisfactory, the bad better, the average outstanding.

In your school, who are the students who lead the class in academic achievement? Who are the students that get A's? They are the students who are dissatisfied with mediocre performance. They are the ones who are constantly trying to make the average outstanding.

This same principle applies to work in the Church. Do you think the Lord is satisfied with anything less than the best? Do you think 50, 70 or even 85 percent attendance at Mutual is satisfactory to him? Do you think that a Church talk that's half prepared and poorly delivered is adequate? Is the Lord satisfied with a home teaching "visit" that is conducted over the phone or on the street corner?

The Lord expects from us a constant striving for perfection in all things. To achieve that perfection we need leaders who are not satisfied with the ordinary. We need leaders who are 100 percent committed and dedicated to the kingdom. If you will remain, so to speak, cheerfully unsatisfied while continually reaching for perfection, you will be an effective leader and realize progress as a reward for your efforts.

There are many traits common among leaders, but there is one quality which is inevitable in every leader — leaders are goal-setters. It is impossible to lead anyone anywhere if you don't know yourself where you're going.

I once heard a story about a young sophomore in college who invited several of his friends from his dormitory to come to his home for the Thanksgiving holiday. The boys were to travel in two cars. An additional friend, learning of their intended journey and the available room, asked if he could ride with the boys as far as his hometown. After they had dropped this boy off they then had to take a slightly different route home than the road the host student usually traveled.

After the boys had been driving for quite a long time along a backwoods road through desolate country, the fellows in the second car began to get worried about whether they were on the right road. They signaled to the driver of the first car to pull over.

"Have you got a road map?" they asked.

"No," the host replied.

"And you've never taken this road home?" they inquired.

"Nope," he answered.

"Then how do you know you're on the right road? We're lost, aren't we?"

"No," the student calmly answered. "See that electric wire?" he asked, pointing to a high-tension electric line overhead. "I've had my eye on that all along. It goes right to my hometown."

And sure enough a few minutes later the two carloads of boys arrived at that town.

Before you can lead others, you too must have a destination — a goal — and you must have some guidelines to follow in achieving your goal. In the game of football the goal is to score touchdowns. But touchdowns aren't made by accident. They are scored because the players, led by a coach, have established prior guidelines, or plays, which help them accomplish their goal. As a leader you need to set goals and to have a master plan to achieve them.

President Lee once said, "It is difficult to follow a leader who isn't going anywhere." I hope you're not that kind of a leader. If you're a quorum or class president, where are you going? What goals have you established for your class? for your personal growth? You have to set goals at the beginning of the year. Decide to fellowship and reactivate Steve, to learn how to macrame and crochet, to help Sister Jarman with her Saturday chores, to run a five-minute mile, and so on. Otherwise, at the end of the year you'll be just where you started — nowhere.

Let me share one of my favorite quotations about leadership, which comes from the Hillsdale College Leadership Letter of December 1965 - January 1966. "Leadership begins with a desire to achieve. To achieve, the leader must set goals. To set goals he must make decisions. To achieve goals he must plan. To plan he must analyze. To implement he must organize. To organize he must delegate. To delegate he must administer. To administer he must communicate. To communicate he must motivate. To motivate he must share. To share he must care. To care he must believe. To believe he must set goals that inspire belief and the desire to achieve. Thus the process of leadership begins and ends with goals."

But leadership is more than just directing others. The ability to administer and delegate is an important facet of leadership; but, in the Church context particularly, service is the most important part. Note how the Savior taught this principle. At the feast of the passover just prior to his betrayal, he rose from the table, poured water into a basin, and began to wash the disciples' feet. Peter protested, saying, "Thou shalt never wash my feet." But the Savior answered, "If I wash thee not, thou hast no part with me." (John 13:8.) After the Savior had concluded his act of love he said to the disciples: "If I then, your Lord and Master, have washed your feet; ye also ought to wash one another's feet. For I have given you an example, that ye should do as I have done to you. Verily, verily, I say unto you, The servant is not greater than his lord; neither he that is sent greater than he that sent him." (John 13:14-16.)

From this incident we can see that to be a true leader in the kingdom a person must cultivate a sincere desire to serve others. As the Savior put it: "And whosoever will be chief among you, let him be your servant." (Matthew 20:27.)

Good leadership is like trying to move a piece of string across a table. If you push the string from one end it will bend and buckle, curve and sway. But if you take hold of the other end and gently pull the string, it will follow straight behind. Good leaders are not pushers from behind; they are out ahead, doing their share and serving those they lead.

Those who have risen to positions of leadership, whether in the Church, community or country, have demonstrated the validity of this principle. Theodore Roosevelt was once decorating one of his soldiers for bravery in the Spanish-American War. He said: "This is the bravest man I have ever seen. He walked right behind me all the way up San Juan Hill."

As a leader you are going to be as carefully observed by those you direct as a diamond is by a potential buyer. The diamond buyer scrutinizes the diamond for flaws in clarity such as black carbon spots. He checks for color; perfect diamonds are completely colorless. And most importantly, he checks to see that the stone has been properly proportioned and cut so that every facet reflects light.

Those who follow you will look to see what you reflect. Will they find in you the flaws of false pride and self-aggrandizement? Are you a leader just to make yourself appear greater in the eyes of your peers? Or will they find in you a righteous person who is leading out to help accomplish the work of the Lord? As they examine you will they be impressed to follow you because you are sincere in your intent? Do your actions and your words speak the same message? As a leader your words are empty and meaningless if your actions reflect a life contrary to your teachings.

Unfortunately many members of the Church rationalize and attempt to excuse their own faults and inadequacies because of the actions of some Church leaders. For leaders to be truly effective they must be like a perfectly clear diamond. They must be pure in heart, as discussed in detail in chapter 15. This means they must rid themselves of all inclinations toward evil. As you do this you will develop a strength of character and integrity which will make you a leader worthy of examination and emulation. You will no longer have any disposition toward evil but will only desire to do good continually and to serve others.

Lastly, and most importantly, be humble. Someone has said, "A good leader takes a little more than his share of the blame and a little less than his share of the credit." Don't think because you have a leadership position that you are better than those you serve. I found this statement in an issue of the Royal Bank of Canada monthly letter: "He is a wise man who does not allow himself to be elated by the things he comes to possess. When a man becomes eminent, he should carry his honors with gentleness, magnanimity, and absence of arrogance. Guard against allowing success to go to your head, or the tightness of your halo may cause headaches."

You will not become impressed by your own importance if you recognize your limitations and inadequacies. Realize that just because you have attained a position of leadership it does not mean that you can now "retire." Constantly try to make yourself a better leader. Don't let yourself become obsolete. Keep learning. Just as your blood supplies your body with oxygen and nutrients necessary for growth, knowledge nourishes your mind with the elements necessary for fresh new thought and activity. Allow knowledge, not success, to go to your head.

What a bearing leadership ability has on your do-it-yourself destiny! Prepare now to lead and you will be taking a giant step forward. And as you do, remember the messages of this chapter:

1. Be a leader who is a good follower, a leader who has not sought high places but who has been drafted into leadership because of his ability and willingness to serve in any capacity.

2. Be a leader who is willing to discipline himself, who is willing to pay the price of leadership.

3. Be a leader who is dissatisfied with the average; keep your head in the clouds but your feet on the ground.

4. Be a leader who sets goals; know where you're going, why you are going, and how to get there.

5. Be a leader who considers leadership an opportunity to serve.

6. Be a leader who leads for the good of those concerned and not for your own personal gratification.

7. Be a leader who is humble.

Seek to incorporate these seven points into your life. Work at them. Then the next time you hear the word "leader" you will immediately think, "That's me!"

11

Of Mind
and Muscle

There are many people in this life I feel sorry for. Some of them are sick all the time; others have crippling handicaps; others just seem to run into all kinds of afflictions. But there is a kind of person who has a mental rather than a physical impairment, one that does not show on his face or body but which definitely handicaps him as he goes through life. For this person too I feel very sorry. It is the person who has never learned to enjoy work.

In the extreme case the very word *work* strikes fear to the heart and spreads a pallor over the cheeks. Further up the scale are those who work when they must, who more or less endure work as a duty, as a necessary evil in life. But the person who gets real joy out of life is the one who gets real joy out of work. This may not be the easiest concept to comprehend, but believe me when I say that it is true. There are few acquisitions that will be more important to you as you grow older than the power to work and enjoy it.

I am reminded of the story about Thomas Edison, who day after day worked long hours in his laboratory bringing to exciting reality the inventions which his creative genius had dreamed up. So intense was his application and so long his hours that those close to him became concerned for his health and well-being. "Why don't you take a vacation?" they asked. "What you ought to do is just go to the place where most of all you would like to and there do what you would really like to do." Edison agreed to do this, starting the next day. True to his promise, early the next morning he was found in his laboratory, working.

There are those who find their work boring. Of course, we have to admit that some types of work are naturally more fulfilling to the individual than others, and a person should by all means strive to place himself in satisfying work. But isn't a feeling of boredom, like a sense of fulfillment, largely a condition of the mind rather than a position of the body? And a condition of the mind, a mental attitude, can always be changed by the same mind that originally generated it.

Those who have suffered the depths of enforced boredom will tell you that, far from being a producer of boredom, physical and mental effort is the greatest cure for boredom that exists. Consider, for instance, the men who returned from prison camps in North Vietnam a few years back, some of whom had endured that imprisonment for seven or eight years. Not only were the physical conditions of the prisons primitive but the authorities deliberately kept the men unoccupied.

Housed largely in single or double cells and permitted no official communication with other prisoners, allowed no periods for exercise, deprived of every scrap of reading material, these men would have gone crazy if they had not worked out for themselves some way to occupy time profitably. They took exercise in their own skimpy cells — push-ups, sit-ups, running on the spot, and so on. They devised a code system by which to communicate with each other between cells. They raked their brains for things they had learned, and then taught these subjects to others. How they would have loved to have some productive work to do! They saved their sanity by occupying their waking hours in putting forth physical and mental effort to the greatest extent possible — that is, by working. This is the way they conquered boredom.

How shall we assess work as a principle? Well, let me suggest that work is an eternal principle. Even before the Fall, Adam was placed in the Garden of Eden and told to dress it and keep it, which means that he had to perform some measure of work. Here the Lord was recognizing that Adam would have been miserable if he had just done nothing. After the Fall and the cursing of the ground so that it brought forth thorns and thistles, there came the command, "In the sweat of thy face shalt thou eat bread, till thou return unto the ground." Here the Lord named work as a principle of life. I notice too that he placed no mortal time-limit upon a man's work span. Ideally he would work during his entire life. Retirement at sixty-five or at any other predetermined age is a principle of man, not of God.

Nor should we reckon on putting our feet up and resting when we get to the other side. We know that the work of the kingdom is being pushed forward in the spirit world just as it is on earth. In his great vision on the redemption of the dead, President Joseph F. Smith saw that righteous elders, when they leave this mortal life, engage in missionary work there. Beyond the resurrection the same story applies, it would seem. In fact, there may sometimes be an even greater intensity to the work when our mortal life is over. President Wilford Woodruff had an interesting story to tell about this, a vision he received years after the death of the Prophet Joseph Smith.

"Joseph Smith continued visiting myself and others up to a certain time, and then it stopped. The last time I saw him was in heaven. In the night vision I saw him at the door of the temple in heaven. He came and spoke to me. He said he could not stop to talk with me because he was in a hurry. I met a half dozen brethren who had held high positions on earth and none of them could stop to talk with me because they were in a hurry. I was much astonished.

"By and by, I saw the Prophet again, and I got the privilege to ask him a question. 'Now,' said I, 'I want to know why you are in a hurry. I have been in a hurry all through my life, but I expected my hurry would be over when I got into the Kingdom of Heaven, if I ever did.'

"Joseph said, 'I will tell you, Brother Woodruff; every dispensation that has had the priesthood on the earth and has gone into the celestial kingdom has had a certain amount of work to do to prepare to go to the earth with the Savior when he goes to reign on the earth. Each dispensation has had ample time to do this work. We have not. We are the last dispensation, and so much work has to be done and we need to be in a hurry in order to accomplish it.'

"Of course, that was satisfactory with me, but it was new doctrine to me."

As a further point on the eternity of the principle of work, can you imagine God himself and our Savior sitting around in heaven throughout the eternities doing nothing? Surely it must take much mental effort to organize and control the great creations they have made and are making, to people worlds, to ensure that God's children on those worlds are educated in righteous principles, and so on. And you only have to read section 76 of the Doctrine and Covenants to recognize that all who expect or hope to find a place in the kingdom of heaven, as well as willing souls in lower kingdoms, will be actively engaged in the work of bringing about God's eternal purposes.

To use a modern expression, "If you can't beat them, join them." Translated into our present context, this means that since work is a glorious, inescapable and eternal principle, it would be well for each of us to thoroughly cultivate its acquaintance and thereby learn to enjoy its company. We will then come to recognize that the "curse" of work placed upon Adam and his posterity was in effect a great blessing, that it was more a challenge of opportunity than a commandment of punishment.

Since what we are talking about is basically a mental attitude, make your attitude toward work enthusiastic. Whatever the work, be it school work, after-school work, work at home, or regular daily work, start it each day with vigor and gusto rather than with an "I suppose I must" approach. This will develop within you the desire to give rather than take, the wish to contribute rather than deplete. The quantity and quality of the work you accomplish, as well as the satisfaction you get out of it, will be greatly increased by this attitude.

Regrettably, that positive, want-to-contribute approach apparently is on the decline these days. Some years ago, before being called as a General Authority, I had the privilege of serving as the corporate training director for a large chain of grocery stores. I was very proud to be thought worthy of that position in that fine company, and I was diligent to see that as far as possible we recruited and trained personnel who would be a credit to the company. Yet frequently when young people came in to the personnel department to fill out an application for employment, even before they had completed the form they would be inquiring what benefits the company would give them. "How many days' vacation do I get a year? How many holidays? Do we get a rest break in the morning and afternoon? How long is our lunch period?"

So the questions would go on, showing tremendous concern about the possible benefits the company would offer and never once indicating what the would-be employee intended to do for the company. Rarely did an applicant exhibit an attitude which said: "I'll work my heart and soul out for this company. I simply want to go to work, and I promise you I will earn my own way." Noticeably lacking was the attitude: "I'll give you mental and physical ambition. I'll try to be creative at my job. I'll try to be public-relations conscious. I feel that I have a contribution to make and I'm anxious to make it. I need the job, and I promise you that if I get it I'll be honest, I'll be loyal, and I will not disappoint your organization." Much more usually the applicant would obviously be concerned solely with what he could get out of the job. I need hardly say which kind of applicant had the best chance of getting a job, assuming that we had a choice.

In work as in other aspects of our lives, the words of President Harold B. Lee seem to me to hit the mark — "The greatest poverty is the poverty of desire." I believe that with all my heart. When someone said, "You are the light on the hill, either for good or for evil," he made a true statement. As Church members we are supposed to be the light. Collectively speaking, no other organization has the discipline, government, and order that the Church has. Traditionally our people are trained to work. The Church was built upon a combination of faith and work. It will be for you, my young friends, to maintain and extend this tradition as you get older, and the time to absorb and assimilate and practice this principle is now.

The poor, negative attitude to a person's daily work frequently begets disloyalty. In a measure the poor attitude itself is an act of disloyalty, but sometimes in addition the employee will be perpetually critical of his boss, will tear down the company he works for when in the company of friends, and so on. Elbert Hubbard had a few words to say on this topic, and I like and agree with every one of them.

"I think if I worked for a man, I would work for him. I would not work for him part of the time and the rest of the time work against him. I would give him an undivided service or none. If put to the pinch, an ounce of loyalty is worth a pound of cleverness. If you must vilify, condemn, and eternally desparage, why, resign your position. And when you are outside, damn to your heart's content. But I pray you, so long as you are part of an institution, do not condemn it. Not that you will injure the institution; not that, but when you disparage the concern of which you are a part, you disparage yourself. More than that, you are loosening the tendrils which hold you to the institution, and the first high wind that comes along, you will be uprooted and blown away in a blizzard's track and probably you will never know why."

I am fortunate in being one of those to whom enthusiasm for work comes easily. It was while I was attending junior high school that I started my first work for an employer, a five-store grocery company in Salt Lake City. I worked there for eight years — all the way through junior high school, through high school, and then for a couple of years after graduation. Around that time Albertson's Food Centers came to Salt Lake City. I recognized that they were not just a local firm and that employment with them might increase my chances for promotion. I determined that I would seek employment with Albertson's.

I made an appointment to see the district manager the next day, and that evening I went home and discussed the matter with my wife. Then I went to bed and discussed it with myself all night. I don't think I slept at all that night. Everything was hanging on tomorrow's interview, and I knew I didn't have the confidence I needed; yet I had to sell myself and get the job because I was very anxious to work for that particular company. I prepared for the interview through the night. I went over it a thousand times, visualizing one by one the questions that would be asked me and responding to them in many different ways through the long night. I wouldn't say I was confident when the morning came, but I believe I was prepared.

Let me digress from the story a moment to give a word of counsel. When you go to look for a job, go looking your best. Don't go in your grubbies, for example. Go as if you are looking for a job in earnest, as indeed you should be. You not only need to work at working, but when you don't have a job you need to work at *looking* for work. Don't go out with the attitude that you'll answer this one particular ad and then go home again. You have nothing more important to do than get lined up with some kind of work. Work at the problem eight or ten hours a day until you get a job.

Back to my story. I had only one suit at that time, a gray suit, so I wore it, shined my shoes well, dressed to look the best I possibly could. I had to wait quite a long time in the office before the district manager finally had time to interview me. We questioned and answered back and forth for about twenty minutes. Then he said, "Well, the best we can offer you is $68 for a forty-hour week." (This was way back in 1954.) At the time I was making $107 a week in my current job. I explained the situation — that I very much wanted to work for Albertson's but that $68 would mean too big a cut in my present income. We talked a bit longer and then he made another offer. "Well, I think maybe we can go to $78 for a forty-hour week."

I knew that I just couldn't get by on that figure. Already my wife and I had only barely enough money to pay the mortgage each month, and to make things worse my car had broken down. At the level of income now proposed, how would I even make ends meet, let alone make any progress? How was I going to take care of my tithing and other contributions I felt I needed to give to the Church?

We talked briefly again. Finally the district manager said: "I'll tell you what we'll do. We'll give you $78 a week plus eight hours of overtime, which will total about $104 a week. That is absolutely the most we can give. We are only paying our department head $110. Now, you go home and decide whether you want to work for us on this basis and we'll decide whether we want to hire you."

I went home. On the way I convinced myself that twelve dollars a month less income wasn't much to worry about in view of the opportunities I would get in working for a larger company. Twelve dollars *was* a lot, however, compared with our scanty salary at that time. I told my wife: "I'm going to work for Albertson's. Will you support me?" She said she would.

The next morning I went down to my old job and worked just as I normally did. At 9:00 A.M., as the store opened, in walked five of the executives from Albertson's Food Center. They walked down through the produce department, of which I was co-manager, examined it, said "Hello" to me, and then left the store. A short while later one of them phoned me and said, "We would like to hire you." "How soon?" I asked. "On October 4," was the reply.

It was then about the middle of May. This meant that I had to work on at my old job for about five months, all the time keeping secret the fact that I would be leaving to take up a new job. All the time too I must maintain my enthusiasm for the present job. It was one of the difficult tests of my life, but I made it.

When I finally went to work for Albertson's I really did try to work hard. I wanted to make my way in the company as fast as I could, and obviously the way to do that was to impress my employers with my willingness and ability to work. This attitude of mine led to one or two incidents which in retrospect may look a little amusing but at the time might have gone the other way.

The store had a turnstile that was in need of repair. It not only let people into the grocery department as designed, but it also let them out again — that is, the lock was broken and it would turn either way. Those of us who were working on the racks in the store would run up through this turnstile and push through it the wrong way to make our way to the checkstands whenever one of the checkers called out for assistance. One night, however, the turnstile was repaired, but the manager did not think to let all the staff know about the repair. Not knowing that the turnstile was now locked against inside traffic attempting to get out, when someone called for help up front I took off on a dead run and hit the turnstile in the usual way, only to find that it locked in place. I pulled it out of the floor and carried it about ten feet over to the soda fountain area where the district manager was sitting — the man who had hired me. I remember laying it down on the floor and saying, "Oops, sorry!"

About two weeks later, I achieved another smashing success of a similar kind. I was running in from the parking lot after having taken out a customer's groceries, and when I hit the front door it came off its hinges. I carried it right on in and laid in down. It must have weighed 150 pounds or so. You might guess that sitting at the checkstand was — yes, the district manager? Almost my first thought at that point was that the company couldn't afford to have me working for them. But fortunately that manager could see beyond that. He could see that I was trying hard and was working for success; and any employer is bound to be delighted with that kind of attitude in an employee.

I suppose that people get most enthusiastic about their work when they are doing work they like to do. Doing what you like as work may not always be possible, but if that's not practicable for you I believe that the next best thing usually is — liking what you do. There are ways to improve that "liking," thereby adding zest and enjoyment to the job and making it more productive not only for the employer but also for the worker. One technique for this is the use of the creative approach.

Virtually every job could be done more efficiently than it is being done now. As you work, analyze in your head the goal of your efforts and devise better and faster ways to achieve it. Even the simplest improvements can sometimes make a difference to output. Would a larger sledge-hammer break up this concrete faster? Could those boxes be stacked in less space if turned the other way? If the tape machine were on the other side of me, could I seal these boxes faster? Could I increase my output at the desk if I rearranged my work so as to handle the more routine matters later in the day, dealing with the more creative ones earlier when my mind is fresher? Almost any job will respond to the power of creative thought; and the effect is not only to upgrade work efficiency but also to improve the worker's mental development and his interest in and enjoyment of the work.

Linked with the creative, enthusiastic approach is the desire and ability to see the big picture. In those earlier grocery-store days I would think of myself not merely as stacking bags of potatoes on a rack but as helping to feed a community. Shipping clerks in an LDS publishing firm may see themselves either as packing books in boxes or as helping to spread the truths of the gospel. The story of the two men working at different ends of the large construction project is a familiar one. Asked what he was doing, one said he was mixing mortar. The other man, involved in the same process, replied that he was building a cathedral. Attitude of mind and heart has as much effect upon work as upon any other aspect of our lives.

As another way to add interest and enjoyment to the job, compete with yourself, set goals which demand from you an increase of speed or efficiency. As you achieve one goal, set a higher one for next time. In this way, once again you will not only be serving the company better but you will also be training yourself, and any training is someday going to result in better skills and probably in a better job.

So work at liking your job, and you will end up with bigger dividends even than an improved day-to-day situation at work, important as that may be. Work well done gives the doer a sense of accomplishment and achievement. This in turn brings a zest for further work and greater accomplishment. Fortunately there is no limit to the possibilities. We climb one hill and another one comes into view.

The story of Tommy expresses the concept simply. Tommy was about five years old and was showing a visitor some of his drawings — birds, dogs, cars, houses. He confided that these were not his best drawings. "May I see your best drawings, then?" asked the visitor. "Oh," replied Tommy, "I haven't done those yet."

While reaching for a constantly rising standard of work, when you have obtained the formal training in your chosen career you should aspire to the best type of job within that field. I was impressed by what Elder Joseph Anderson said once in a meeting of the General Authorities in the temple. "Having trained to be a shorthand writer, I knew that that was what I was going to be all my life — a secretary. And since I would be writing shorthand all my life, I determined to have the finest job in the world which required the use of shorthand. Where was that? Of course, it was working for the First Presidency of the Church." Brother Anderson served for fifty years as secretary to the First Presidency. During all of those years he had almost daily contact with the prophets, with the greatest men alive. He had indeed chosen the finest job in his field.

Although you may expect to do better work in the future as your talents and skills improve and as the challenges and opportunities increase, never do less than your currently best work right now. There is always an immediate reward in work well done, in the shape of self-approval and of that sense of accomplishment we have already talked about. The rewards last longer than that, however, showing up repeatedly if subconsciously in the solution of future problems based on the experience gained.

The famous Daniel Webster had an unusual experience

wherein the reward, though delayed, was very specific. Mr. Webster related this incident during a conversation about the importance of doing small things thoroughly and to the best of one's ability. He said that when he was a young lawyer a small insurance case was brought to him in which only a small amount was involved and for which his fee was to be only twenty dollars. The story continues:

"He saw that, to do his clients full justice, a journey to Boston, to consult the law library, would be desirable. He would be out of pocket by such an expedition, and for his time he would receive no adequate compensation. After a little hesitation he determined to do his very best, cost what it might. He accordingly went to Boston, looked up the authorities, and gained the case.

"Years after this, Webster, then famous, was passing through New York City. An important insurance case was to be tried the day after his arrival, and one of the counsel had been suddenly taken ill. Money was no object, and Webster was begged to name his terms and conduct the case.

" 'I told them' said Mr. Webster, 'that it was preposterous to prepare a legal argument at a few hours' notice. They insisted, however, that I should look at the papers; and this, after some demur, I consented to do. Well, it was my old twenty-dollar case over again, and as I never forget anything, I had all the authorities at my fingers' ends. The Court knew that I had had no time to prepare, and was astonished at the range of my acquirements. So, you see, I was handsomely paid both in fame and money for that journey to Boston; and the moral is that good work is rewarded in the end, though, to be sure, one's self-approval should be enough.' "

I am by no means a Daniel Webster, but my experience teaches me that there are always monetary rewards for the person who will work hard. When I went to work for Albertson's, I gave them my best and hardest work. Fifteen months after I started working for them, I received a promotion which made me supervisor of one of the districts, meaning that I would now supervise several stores. My experiences with that company indicate to me a success formula. I don't know exactly how I picked it up or whether it is a personal thing, but I believe it. I call it the eight-, twelve-, or fifteen-hour formula. It goes like this: If you work hard for eight hours a day, your major promotion will come in about ten years; if you work hard for twelve hours a day, your major promotion will come in about five years; and if you work hard for fifteen hours a day, giving it your whole heart and soul, your promotion will come in fifteen months to two years. I really believe this formula. I have watched man after man apply it, and I know that as a general rule it works.

How should you work, then? Hard, fast, not being afraid to push yourself to greater efforts which in turn will increase your capacity to work. This applies whether you are working on a family project, working for yourself, working for an employer, or working in a Church position. Bear in mind too that it applies to both physical and mental work. It applies just as much when you are studying for school work, for example, as when you are digging a ditch or when you are pulling weeds in the family garden.

I am referring to the fact that when you work fast and hard and intensely at your studying, it becomes a habit. Thereafter, every time you study you do so with the intensity developed in your habit. When you read, you read in that habitual way. This intensity spills over into the physical area from the mental, and vice versa. In either case you work hard and fast because you have made it a habit. On the other hand, if you have developed the habit of slothfulness and laziness, that habit too stays with you so that every time you work you do so at that same slow pace. Your accomplishments are then lowered. You miss the excitement of it all, the excitement of working fast, thinking fast and, as I believe, thinking clearer.

In a previous book *A Generation of Excellence* I reproduced a poem which gives the modern version of "The Little Red Hen." That poem tells of the big red rooster who was so intent on grumbling about poor conditions that he neglected to work and went to bed supperless; whereas the diligent little red hen merely dug faster and deeper and was rewarded by a stomachful of worms.

This story is true in its connotations. It's the "little red hens" who get the work done. You don't have to be a genius or a great intellectual to be in the ranks of the little red hens. Many students of average intelligence and a normal IQ have a high performance level because they have learned how to work. I believe that work is a skill, an attitude, a habit, and many other things. Some young people have developed it to the point that they will do whatever it takes to get the job done. These are the ones who end up with superior grades, in many cases with better grades than those with higher IQs. They are also the ones who get the better jobs.

And while we are talking about the habit of working hard, we must remember that even working hard is sometimes not enough. An exceptional need sometimes calls for exceptional effort.

Some years ago a little girl named Kathy, while playing on a vacant lot, fell into a large pipe. She was down many, many feet in the pipe. Rescue operations were conducted, and I recall reading in the newspaper reports of the occasion that there was one steamshovel operator who worked for something like sixty-seven hours without a break. That is almost three full days, night and day. What was his goal? To get out the poor little frightened soul in the bottom of the pipe. Unfortunately when they finally got her out she was dead. But that man had worked all those long hours to try to save her.

There will be times in your life when you must work those kinds of hours under that kind of pressure to save a soul or otherwise to do something which, although it may not be done against such a dramatic background, nevertheless must be done as a matter of urgency.

And now I'll let you into a little secret. First of all a question: What do you think is the hardest work we can do? You may be thinking of all kinds of physical labor, but I would say that *controlled thinking* is the hardest thing we can do. The mind works all of the time, twenty-four hours a day every day, either subconsciously or consciously. But unless it is disciplined it is not selective; it will reach out and grasp anything that is nearby or is in the memory and will think on it. Be sure to control and discipline your thinking, because however hard may be the work of controlled thinking, the alternative of uncontrolled thought represents a great waste of mental powers. I believe it was Dr. Hugh Nibley who said, "Our mind will take a terrible revenge if we do not think constructive things."

Improving work attitudes and habits, then, involves not only physical ambition but also mental ambition. Life would be unbalanced if all our work was simply physical — or, for that matter, was all mental. To my mind, toiling on a farm or in the yard until the perspiration pours off you is a great purging experience. The mind also needs to go through that same kind of purging now and again. We need to think so fiercely sometimes that our head almost aches. Most of us have been involved in some pretty intense thinking at times, usually the night before final exams. Increasingly we need to go through that kind of a process, wherein we feel that totally controlled, focused, intent thinking is taking place. When such a process is over, there comes a refreshing feeling, a feeling of accomplishment and peace in contrast to the exertion we have just put forth.

The ability to totally control thinking is not a common acquirement. A man who comes readily to mind in this connection is President N. Eldon Tanner of the First Presidency. He and the other Brethren of the First Presidency have to make many decisions based on the presentations of others, and consequently President Tanner sits in meetings hour after hour listening. He has an outstanding ability to listen. He closes his eyes as he does so, so that you would almost think he was asleep. But he is far from asleep. He is concentrating. His thinking is focused so much upon what is being said that occasionally he will stop the speaker and ask, "Did I understand what you just said?" Then he will review the speaker's words. By this rare ability he has corrected many potential mistakes.

Actually, if you will just think of it for a moment, you will realize that there is no aspect of the life of a true Latter-day Saint which does not involve working in some degree, either physically or mentally. It is equally evident that true prayer, the fervent, dedicated prayer that secures the needed answer, similarly represents a considerable effort. Read again the prayer experience of Enos in the Book of Mormon — notice that he did not merely get down on his knees and pray intently for five minutes, ten minutes, or even half an hour. He prayed all the day long and was still praying when night fell. Have you ever prayed with all of your heart and soul? Have you ever really needed something when it was as if you were confronted with a wall too high, too long and too deep to go over, around or under, but nevertheless you had to get to the other side? I have been in these circumstances a few times in my life, and I want to tell you that at such times you really learn how to plead with the Lord. And in doing so you make a tremendous mental and spiritual effort.

If all that I have said in this chapter makes you think that life is a lot of work, I have managed to get the message over. If what I have said depresses you, I have not. I say again that my experience from my youth up teaches me of the great value of work both physical and mental, and of the tremendous enjoyment and sense of accomplishment that can come from it. I have tried to share these concepts and feelings with you because of the great importance of the subject, particularly in a time when these concepts are losing ground in society. This principle of work is just as much a principle of the gospel as is any other good principle. Consequently it will endure forever. Consequently too, as with all other gospel principles, incorporating it into life will bring nothing but happiness and joy.

So let me reverse the statement I made in the first paragraph of this chapter. Let me say that there are many people in this life I feel happy for. Those are the people who have learned to enjoy work; for those are the people who have learned to enjoy life.

12

Your Building
Standards

Picture this. It's summertime and you and your family have just moved into a brand new home. The walls still smell of fresh paint. The carpeting is thick and plush; the cabinets are built of beautiful oak. Everything that meets the eye appears to be of the finest quality. But as the seasons change, the first winter storm hits. A strong gust of wind blows in the windows, then a wet sleet washes the mortar from between the bricks. Finally the sleet turns to snow — and the weight of the snow caves the roof in.

Thank goodness such disasters don't occur! Thank goodness that when a contractor builds a home he knows the hardships which Mother Nature will impose and fortifies the home against her forces. Over the years these fortifications and precautions have developed into what we now call a building code. Standards have been established to govern the quality of materials and workmanship in a home in order to prevent such disasters from occurring. Those who are wiser and more experienced in the field of home construction have designed these building codes to protect those who are less knowledgeable.

You too are subject to the rigors of the world. What prevents you from collapsing under the weight of the world's forces? Let's look at the project of building you.

Members of the Church are constantly being reminded that we should be in the world but not of the world. What does this mean? Elder Bruce R. McConkie defines the "world" as "the social conditions created by such of the inhabitants of the earth as live carnal, sensuous, lustful lives, and who have not put off the natural man by obedience to the laws and ordinances of the gospel."

John described the "world" as "the lust of the flesh, and the lust of the eyes, and the pride of life." (1 John 2:16.) He said:

"Love not the world, neither the things that are in the world. If any man love the world, the love of the Father is not in him.

"For all that is in the world, the lust of the flesh, and the lust of the eyes, and the pride of life, is not of the Father, but is of the world.

"And the world passeth away, and the lust thereof; but he that doeth the will of God abideth for ever." (1 John 2:15-17.)

Obviously, then, the "world" does not refer to this earth on which we live but to the environment created by individuals who live contrary to the teachings of the Savior.

Life is a probationary state. It was necessary for us to come to earth to gain a body. We must therefore be in the world. But as Latter-day Saints we do not have to be of the world or, in other words, part of the evil environment of the world.

Just as standards have been established to protect new home buyers from the elements of the world, standards have been established to protect you from the evils of the world. Those who are wiser and more experienced have established building codes to help ensure a quality product when the project of building you is complete. What are some of these standards?

For one, Latter-day Saint youth have been asked to refrain from dating until they are sixteen years of age. This counsel is given to help keep you from the evils of the world. President Spencer W. Kimball gave this advice in a talk entitled "Save the Youth of Zion" delivered in 1965 at June Conference. He said: "Early dating, especially early steady dating, brings numerous problems, much heartache, and numerous disasters. The early date often develops into the steady date, and the steady date frequently brings on early marriage, of which there are hun-

dreds of thousands with sixteen- and seventeen-year-old
brides. Early marriages often end in disillusionment, frustration, and divorce, with broken homes and scarred lives. Far
more high-school marriages end in divorce than marriages of
more mature young people. Dating, and especially steady dating, in the early teens is most hazardous. It distorts the whole
picture of life. It deprives the youth of worthwhile and rich
experiences. It limits friendships and reduces acquaintances
which can be so valuable in selecting a partner for time and
eternity."

Many youth have asked: "I have nonmember friends who
are permitted to date at fifteen. Why can't I?" Perhaps the
simplest answer is found in some very wise advice from
Ecclesiastes: "To every thing there is a season, and a time to
every purpose under the heaven." (Ecclesiastes 3:1.) The teenage years constitute a season for growing, a season in which you
begin to change from a boy or girl to a young man or woman,
change not only physically but emotionally. Physical maturity,
however, does not necessarily mean that a person is emotionally
mature enough to handle a one-boy-one-girl dating relationship.

I recall a mother who visited her bishop. She said: "We have
given our daughter permission to date, and she is just fifteen.
She is more mature than other girls her age." Physically she was
more mature than other girls her age, and the mother felt totally
justified in letting this young lady date. Of course the bishop
counseled very strongly against it, but to no avail. Within a short
time the daughter came in alone to see the bishop. She was
heartbroken and carrying a burden of guilt that a person so
young — any person, in fact — should never have to carry.

President Spencer W. Kimball gave this further advice on the
subject of early dating: "When you get in the teenage years, your
social associations should still be general acquaintance with boys
and girls. Any dating or pairing off in social contacts should be
postponed until at least the age of sixteen or older, and even
then there should be much judgment used in selections and in
the seriousness. Young people should still limit the close contacts for several years since the boy will be going on his mission
when he is nineteen years old."

My personal counsel to youth would be to follow the

prophet, obey his counsel, walk in the footsteps he would have you follow, and don't court temptation. In due time you will have the opportunity to date, and at that time you will be more mentally mature and able to handle the new emotions and feelings which may be present.

If your parents have asked you not to date until you are sixteen or later, realize that they are experienced contractors and that they have established this building code for your own good. Because they love you and know you better than anyone else, they want to make sure you are ready to date, ready to withstand the temptation which may be present in a dating relationship. My wife and I have six sons and one daughter. We decided not to permit them to date until they were sixteen. I feel at peace with this decision in my home. Each family head, as part of his overall responsibility for making decisions governing his family, must make this decision too. I would hope that you and your parents will find it in your best interest to follow the Church's guidelines on this, since they are based on an accumulation of experiences encountered by the General Authorities and other Church leaders over the years.

A second area of much concern to your parents and Church leaders is the controversial subject of popular music. Probably every teenager has thought, "Why don't my parents let me listen to what I want to?"

Nearly three hundred years ago Joseph Addison, an English essayist and poet, wrote this statement: "Music is the only sensual gratification in which mankind may indulge to excess without injury to their moral or religious feelings." That statement may have been true in his day, but it is not true in ours. Much of today's music can be injurious to your moral and religious feelings because it is inconsistent with the companionship of the Spirit of the Lord. For this reason wise parents have cautioned you to be discriminating in the type of music you listen to.

By what standards should you evaluate music? First, look at the message. Are lyrics fitting to a Latter-day Saint if they encourage or even condone moral misconduct, drug abuse, Satan-worship, rejection of legal authority, or acts or attitudes contrary to the gospel?

Second, what about the loudness or intensity of the music?

How does it make you feel? If the music agitates a negative emotion or conveys an unrighteous desire, even though the words may be acceptable, is it "healthy" music? The intensity of music affects the emotional responses of those hearing it more than any other factor. This effect can be positive, as one may experience when hearing a rousing rendition of the "Hallelujah Chorus," or it can be negative, as when it evokes improper thoughts and emotions. A negative emotional response is detrimental to a person's spiritual condition.

Naturally no one can legislate in terms of decibels of sound how loud music can be before it exceeds its honorable purpose and becomes a liability to your spiritual senses. If the music is such that it blocks out touch with reality and listeners become intemperate in their behavior, it is too loud.

The subject of music leads to a discussion of a third building standard — dancing. What is the Church standard regarding dancing, especially rock dancing? Why does the Church continue to hold rock dances when there is so much concern over the type of music played, the volume at which it is performed, and the style of dances which are done?

Dancing can be good, clean entertainment — a wholesome, relaxed, pleasurable experience. It can also be a satanic, sensual, degrading experience. If you have been to a Church dance where there was a controversy between a band member and a priesthood authority over the type and volume of music, it was only because the priesthood leader was trying to make the dance of the former type, not the latter. As I have discussed, excessive noise and beat can cause people to lose touch with reality and act immoderately in behavior, in which case the dance no longer is an uplifting, wholesome experience.

Dances of the proper type have long been a part of Latter-day Saint culture. The pioneers held frequent dances as they traveled across the plains. Dancing helped lighten their spirits and strengthen their determination, unity, and love. After David had defeated the Philistines in battle, the scriptures tell us, he "danced before the Lord with all his might." (2 Samuel 6:14.) His was a dance of praise and appreciation.

What about your dancing? Why are you dancing? What do you feel when you dance? How does the music make you act?

Brigham Young said of dancing, "Those that have kept the

covenants and served their god, if they wish to exercise themselves in a way to rest their mind and tire their body, go and enjoy yourselves in a dance and let God be in all your thoughts in this as in all other things and he will bless you." Can you "let God be in all your thoughts in this"?

The Church believes in holding dances, in providing a good environment where young men and women may meet and socialize. Church leaders don't expect that you dance only the fox-trot and waltz at Church dances, but they do expect you to remember who you are. Acquaintance with the latest music fads and dance steps seems to be part of being young. But remember that you are also a Latter-day Saint and as such have been commanded to use moderation in all things. Make your dancing graceful and dignified, not debasing and lustful. Do not do anything which would call undue attention to yourself. Even the waltz can be unbecoming if it is not done with dignity and refinement.

A friend of mine attended a Church dance many years ago, long before the current dance conditions permitted dancing in any manner and in any direction. The accepted standard at that time was to circle the dance floor in anti-clockwise rotation. My friend had taken a nonmember to this particular dance. One man who was present decided not to conform to the expected norm. He backed up in the wrong direction, accidentally tripping my friend's date and sending her sprawling on the floor.

What kind of impression do you suppose she had of Latter-day Saint dances? What would someone think if they viewed one of our dances today? There should never be any doubt but that our Church dances are proper, uplifting experiences.

Support the priesthood authority in charge if he feels it necessary to turn down the band and turn up the lights. He is only trying to create an appropriate environment, one which you can leave feeling refreshed and invigorated, not jaded and unclean.

Now I realize that not every dance you will attend will be sponsored by the Church. You will need to ask yourself again: "How does this dance make me feel? Am I acting as a Latter-day Saint should? Are my emotions under control and my intentions honorable?" If your answers are not positive and you cannot change the environment to make it wholesome, then have the courage to leave it.

A friend of mine was in a cloak room following a non-LDS dance many years ago. He had found the dance to be a refreshing recreational experience, but some of the other men present had not attended the dance with the same purpose in mind. He overheard two men discussing the girls they had met at the dance and their less-than-honorable intentions toward those girls following the dance.

What is your intent when you attend a dance? What do you think about while you are dancing? Although the environment may be proper, you must also analyze how the dance makes you feel, remembering that the accuracy of your feelings as a measurement of right and wrong is determined by how closely you are in tune with your Father in heaven. Always stand in holy places and conduct your life in such a manner that you have the constant companionship of the Spirit of the Lord, then you will have no difficulty in deciding what your standard should be in this matter.

The fourth and final building code I will mention here is the one you most frequently think of in relation to standards — dress standards. Why are they important in the process of building you? Let me relate a few stories.

Eva and Ava were identical twins, identical not only in appearance but in personality and disposition as well. They decided to have a party, but when it came time to dress for their party they realized that they had not specified what was appropriate dress for the occasion. In order to make their female guests feel comfortable in whatever they wore, Eva wore a dress and Ava wore pants. The party was highly successful, but as the guests were leaving, the twins overheard someone say: "I've always thought Eva and Ava were identical in every way, but tonight I saw a difference. Ava was more outgoing, not quite as refined and dignified as Eva."

Could the way they were dressed have made any difference?

Michael and Dennis were best of friends. Their birthdays were only a few weeks apart; each was the youngest child in his family. Because neither had any brothers or sisters living at home, the two became inseparable companions. They were both straight-A students, both very active in the Church, both well liked at church and at school. They were more alike than many brothers.

When they entered college, Dennis tried out for a school play and was given a role as a pirate. Because of the extended run of the play, the director asked Dennis to grow a beard rather than apply spirit gum and false hair every night during the four-week performance schedule. He was also asked to grow out his hair. The play was to open in January, which meant that Dennis had to go home for Christmas with shaggy hair and a rather untidy-looking beard.

The Young Adults in the boys' home stake traditionally held a dance each New Year's Eve. At Sunday School the week prior to the dance, Michael and Dennis asked two girls in the ward to accompany them New Year's Eve. Michael's date accepted; Dennis was refused. On December 30, and after having invited several LDS girls to accompany him, Dennis still did not have a date.

Had Dennis' beard and hair camouflaged his real self?

A huge new apartment complex was built in Salt Lake City. The apartment rented so quickly that the bishop, in whose ward boundaries the complex was located, was not able to personally call on each apartment to determine if the tenants were members of the Church. He solicited the help of several ward members. With a simple questionnaire in hand, the ward members went to each apartment, asked the name of the tenant, and inquired as to whether or not he was a member of The Church of Jesus Christ of Latter-day Saints. It was a cold winter night, and occasionally the members were invited inside, but the majority of interviews were conducted on the doorstep through a partially opened door.

When the canvassing was complete, the members met back at the ward to warm up and enjoy some hot chocolate. As they chatted about the experience, these were some of the most frequent comments: "I knew the answer to my second question, 'Are you LDS?,' before I even asked it." "Even through a four-inch crack in the door it was obvious which ones were Latter-day Saints." "It was so cold outside that some folks just poked their heads out, but that told me plenty."

Are Latter-day Saints becoming a "peculiar people" in the best sense of the term?

Stop and think about these questions and about why the Church stresses proper grooming and dressing. Then let's see if your conclusions concur with mine.

The way we dress has an influence on the way we act. Have you ever worn a clown costume? How did it make you feel? Did the garish colors and blousy pants make you want to act silly, frivolous, jovial? Have you girls ever tried on your mother's wedding dress? How did that make you feel — queenly, gracious, dignified? Clothes do affect our behavior, as illustrated by the story of Eva and Ava. Both girls were lovely and feminine, and certainly both acted with perfect decorum. But because Ava was in pants she tended to act more casual than her sister, and the difference was apparent.

A girl in a dress will usually act more ladylike than one in pants. A boy in a coat and tie will generally act more refined than one in Levi's. This is not to say that you should always wear dresses or coats and ties. For many occasions this clothing is as inappropriate as Levi's and sneakers are for church. But the point is that you need to be conscious of the effect your clothes can have on your behavior, and always be polite and mannerly, regardless of what the dress for the occasion may be.

As you dress, ask yourself two questions. First, are my clothes clean and pressed, neat and tidy? It doesn't matter whether or not your clothes are the very newest styles and conform to the latest fashion fads. What does matter is how they look. Old clothes that are kept clean and pressed can be more attractive than new ones that are dirty and wrinkled.

And second, are my clothes appropriate for the occasion? There is a difference between what is appropriate and what is acceptable. To be acceptable means something is satisfactory or agreeable. To be appropriate means something is proper and suitable. It may be acceptable for your peers to wear faded, "holey" Levi's to a dance, but it is not appropriate. Have the courage to wear the proper clothing, not just acceptable clothing. Leave the grubby Levi's for work and play outdoors, and clean up for school and for church. What is appropriate will always be acceptable, but what is acceptable will not always be appropriate and may be offensive to others.

Young men, as you officiate in the sacred ordinance of the sacrament, dress appropriately. Wear a dress shirt and tie and, if you own one, a sport coat or suit. Young ladies, put on a dress when the occasion calls for one, and always be sure that it is of a reasonable length and modest in appearance. The following statement was issued by the First Presidency as regards women's dress:

"The Church has not attempted to indicate just how long women's or girls' dresses should be nor whether they should wear pant suits or other types of clothing. We have always counseled our members to be modest in their dress, maintaining such standards in connection therewith as would not be embarrassing to themselves and to their relatives, friends and associates.

"We have advised our people that when going to the temple they should not wear slacks or miniskirts, or otherwise dress immodestly. We have not, however, felt it wise or necessary to give instructions on this subject relative to attendance at our Church meetings, although we do feel that on such occasions they should have in mind that they are in the house of the Lord and should conduct themselves accordingly." (*Priesthood Bulletin*, June 1971.)

Now let's discuss Dennis and Michael. As an LDS girl, would you have as readily accepted a date with Dennis as with Michael? What would have been your impression of Dennis had you never seen him before?

Some people have come to associate long hair and beards with hippies, winos and undesirable characters. This association is not always correct, as evidenced by the case of Dennis and Michael. But people are naturally more suspicious of men with long hair. Because the long-hair movement began as a symbol of rebellion, many people tend to think negatively of young men who wear their hair long.

If you are a young man, what does your hair say about you? What do you want people to think of you? The way you wear your hair can be a definite reflection upon you. Have it trimmed to a reasonable length so that it will not bring about criticism or cause anyone to wonder about your character.

Some years ago I interviewed a young man for a mission. He said to me: "I'll cut my hair so I can go on a mission. But doing so will cause me to lose my identity. As soon as I return I will let it grow back!" How ridiculous! Hair length doesn't determine identity. And furthermore, how much more distinctive an identity he would have as a clean-cut, upstanding young man than just another member of the long-haired masses!

But the most sound argument for keeping your hair well groomed is that the prophet has asked us to do it. And what is the value of having a living prophet if we do not abide by his counsel? What finer example do we have to follow than that of a prophet of God?

On one occasion when President Spencer W. Kimball was president of the St. Joseph Stake in Arizona, he was sitting on the stand at a ward conference. He noticed seven little boys on the front row of the chapel. In perfect unison each of the seven boys raised his right leg and put it over their left knee, and then in a few minutes all seven shifted and put their left leg over their right knee. In unison all would brush their hair with their right hand, and then all seven would lean lightly on their wrists and support their faces by their hands. President Kimball thought their antics to be quite amusing until he discovered that they were copying him. Then he realized the sobering importance of being an example worthy of emulation.

The prophet and President of our Church is a man worthy of emulation. He has asked LDS men to follow his example, to keep our hair short. This should be reason enough to do it.

Take a good look at yourself in the mirror. What does your hair look like? What are you wearing? Is your face clean, neatly made-up, shaven? What would someone think if they came to your home taking a survey and you answered the door? Do you look like a Latter-day Saint?

The apostle Peter said, "But ye are a chosen generation, a royal priesthood, an holy nation, a peculiar people; that ye should shew forth the praises of him who hath called you out of darkness into his marvellous light." (1 Peter 2:9.)

What does it mean to be a "peculiar people?" Those ward members conducting that survey found out. Latter-day Saints, as evidenced by the way they look and live in this "perverse and crooked generation" (Deuteronomy 32:5), are deemed "peculiar" by worldly people. But what a wonderful peculiarity that is!

Conformity to dress and grooming standards is one of the

tests the Lord gives us to see if we will follow the counsel of our prophet and to see if we can stand up against the pressures of the world. Of course there are other underlying reasons: immodesty leads to immorality, long hair and grubby clothes open the door to rebellion and invite associations which lead away from the Church. But even if you are not able to recognize all the valid reasons behind dress and grooming standards, abide by them. When Adam was in the Garden of Eden he was told to offer sacrifices. He knew not why, but he obeyed. He was blessed for doing so and soon came to understand the reasons. The same principle is true for you.

The next time winter brings a wet, sleety snowstorm, be grateful that some wise people knew enough to set standards concerning the building of your home. The brick mason may not have known exactly why he should mix so much cement with so much water and so much gravel, but aren't you glad he did? Aren't you glad that the carpenter used good strong 2 x 4s instead of flimsy 1 x 2s when he built your roof frame?

You'll be glad too if in building your life you follow the standards outlined in this chapter, for as the years pass they will help you to be a stalwart and faithful son or daughter of our Heavenly Father.

13

Good and Funny

"Every time a man laughs," said President David O. McKay, "he takes a kink out of the chain of life." What a blessing it is to be able to laugh! How grateful we should be for high-minded, delightful humor!

One of the steps in the building process is acquiring a sense of humor and learning to differentiate between good and bad humor. Richard L. Evans once said: "Always we must distinguish between what is funny and what is merely filthy, and never give the credentials of humor to what is low-minded or immoral."

Perhaps the easiest way to acquire an appreciation for what is good and funny is to understand what is not. I remember an experience involving a young man of about thirteen years of age. This boy loved to be the center of attention and to make people laugh. One night at a special function in our ward cultural hall a boy with cerebral palsy entered. Using two arm canes, the palsied boy walked with great difficulty. His steps were jerky and erratic. His head flew quickly from side to side without control and his speech was slurred and broken. Everyone in the audience had great empathy for the palsied boy — everyone, that is, except the thirteen-year-old youth. This young man saw an opportunity to get a laugh and started mimicking the palsy sufferer. A few boys laughed as he copied every act of the palsied boy, but most did not. Soon the boy stopped making fun and went on with other amusements.

A few minutes later this boy was perched on a six-foot movable wall in the cultural hall. He lost his balance and fell, landing on the back of his head. I turned pale with fear — fear that the Lord may have chosen to teach this young man a lesson. He lay unconscious for a long moment, then slowly opened his eyes. Fortunately he was all right.

The scriptures tell us that God will not be mocked. Although the word there has a slightly different meaning, God would not want his saints to "mock one another." It is unchristian, cruel and immature to make fun of others less fortunate.

It is incomprehensible to me how anyone can be so insensitive or so desirous of attention that he would cruelly jest or make fun of someone else. I am grateful that I was born with a sensitivity that would not permit me to laugh at someone who had physical limitations or who was less fortunate.

When I was growing up my family was very poor. I often had to wear clothes and shoes which were old and out of style. I remember in particular one occasion when I had to wear some clothes that brought me great embarrassment. I told my mother that I refused to go to school, but she made me go anyway. I was conscious of every glance or stare cast in my direction. Thank goodness no one laughed at me or made fun of me.

A sense of humor can be a most valuable building tool, but never acquire that tool at the expense of someone else. Humor can help and heal or harm and hurt. Humor that calls attention to adverse personal attributes and physical features is humor that harms and hurts.

Humor requires wisdom. If everyone in the group cannot laugh and enjoy your humor, then the humor is inappropriate. This is especially true of practical joking. I remember vividly a practical joke of which I was a part. It seemed perfectly innocent at the time, but it hurt a friend of mine very deeply. One day many years ago while I was working in a store, one of the fellows said, "When Hugh comes to work, let's see who can go the longest without talking to him." Hugh arrived a few moments later and no one spoke to him, although some of us waved and tried to be friendly. As the day wore on, Hugh became notice-ably quiet and indrawn, and I realized that what we were doing was adversely affecting him. I finally told him of our practical joke, but he didn't laugh. He was deeply hurt and remained aloof the rest of the day. Hugh eventually overcame the hurt, but whenever I think how thoughtless we were I hurt inside.

Empathy and sensitivity are valuable qualities to possess, especially as they apply to humor. Pray for an empathy and sensitivity towards people which will keep you from thoughtlessly and foolishly hurting others.

As another area of caution, avoid rude, boisterous and ob-noxious behavior in hopes of gaining attention. Don't indulge in loud, harsh laughter; it's distracting and unrefined. Everyone enjoys a good hearty laugh, but loud and penetrating laughter only degrades. We have been cautioned against obnoxious laughter particularly on the Sabbath day — "not with much laughter, for this is sin." (D&C 59:15.) We can succeed in gaining attention with obnoxious behavior and loud laughter, but such attention is never favorable. How much better it is to be polite, refined, clever and witty than it is to be coarse, rude, vicious and indecent!

If laughter of that kind tends to coarseness, what shall we say of the indecent or off-color story? Never indulge in it. It is undignified in the extreme and totally unfit for any son or daughter of our Heavenly Father.

I once heard of a fellow who stood in a cluster of his friends and began to tell a crude, off-color story. As he began, he paused long enough to ask, "Are there any ladies present?" "No," came a voice from the circle, "but there are gentlemen present." The person who gave that reply knew that dirty stories, even though they may have a funny conclusion, are not worthy of hearing or repeating.

One of the worst effects of off-color humor is the insidious way it persists in the subconscious mind. A friend of mine related to me an experience which occurred nearly forty years ago. During his basic training in the army, the sergeant fre-quently used a seven-word phrase when calling attention to a trainee's mistakes. Though the words in this phrase were ac-ceptable in and of themselves, the sergeant used them to imply a crude, off-color connotation. My friend tells me that he has never repeated this phrase, yet it has unfortunately lingered in his subconscious all these years. Sometimes even now, a simple life experience reminiscent of those days of training will bring the phrase flashing through his conscious mind.

Another area to be avoided in jokes is jesting about spiritual matters. Stories which make light of spiritual things do not constitute appropriate humor. If there is any question in your mind as to the appropriateness of a joke or story, you should ask yourself if you would tell it in the presence of the Lord. You might then refrain from telling jokes about the apostle Peter — the "St. Peter" of the jokes about heaven — and about scriptural prophets and our noble first parents, Adam and Eve. And inasmuch as the Lord is no respecter of persons, shouldn't we also avoid racially derogatory jokes and stories? You will never regret not telling an inappropriate story, but you will wish a thousand times you had not told it if it is sacrilegious and in poor taste and thereby offends a listener.

Appropriate humor can be a great tool in doing the Lord's work. Many stake presidents, mission presidents, bishops and General Authorities have an active sense of humor which contributes to their effectiveness in spreading the gospel. I remember a story President Marion G. Romney once told. Evidently, President Romney's father did not want him to study law. His father did not feel that a man could be a lawyer and remain honest. Reflecting upon this, President Romney said: "That reminds me of the story of the man who walked home from work each night just before midnight. His route home took him through a cemetery. One night when the moon was full the man noticed a new tombstone. He went over to it and read these words: 'Here lies John Brown, an honest man, and a lawyer.' The fellow paused, thought a moment, scratched his head and wondered why they had buried all three men in the same grave!"

Humor is an essential quality of life. It can be such an aid in lifting the heart. Abraham Lincoln once said, "With the fearful strain that is on me night and day, if I did not laugh I should die." A little laughter can do so much to uplift those who are burdened, lonely or depressed. I recall hearing Elder Boyd K. Packer quote a humorous verse which lightens the heart.

If you can smile when things go wrong
And say, "It doesn't matter."
If you can laugh off care and woe
And trouble makes you fatter.

If you can keep a happy face
When all around are blue –
Then have your head examined, Bud,
There's something wrong with you!

For one thing I've arrived at
There are no "ands" or "buts"
The guy that's grinning all the time
Must be completely nuts.

Humor keeps us from taking life too seriously. It is well for us to be able to laugh a little at our problems.

Humor is also a valuable tool for making people feel relaxed in tense, uneasy situations. Whether it's a social gathering or a Church auxiliary meeting, a little story such as the two which follow will make people laugh and feel more comfortable.

Abe Gardner and his wife were home alone one night. Their family was reared and gone. She was knitting and he was reading the paper. After several minutes he put down the paper, looked at his wife, then got a little melancholy and said, "You know, I'm just kind of proud of you." Sister Gardner, being a little hard of hearing, looked up from her knitting and said, "Well, I'm getting kind of tired of you, too."

My second story came from Scotland. At the graveside services of Donald Graham, one of the pallbearers, Blackie McGregor, slipped and fell into the open grave, breaking his arm. A newspaperman covering the funeral service and burial reported the incident in this way: "Yesterday at Donald Graham's funeral, Blackie McGregor, one of the pallbearers, slipped into the open grave, fracturing a limb and bringing a gloom over the whole occasion."

If you find yourself in a gloomy situation, remember such humorous stories as these.

As the work of the Lord goes forth, members of the Church

often find themselves attending numerous meetings. Sometimes they begin early in the morning and they go till late at
night. Before I was called as a General Authority, when I conducted meetings I sometimes opened by telling them the story of
the new convert in California. This convert, amazed at the
number of meetings requiring his attendance, was called on to
speak. He began:

> *Mary had a little lamb*
> *It grew to be a sheep*
> *And then it joined the Mormon Church*
> *And died from lack of sleep.*

Every busy member of the Church can relate to this humorous
verse, and a little laugh will get your meeting started on the right
track.

Speakers often use humor to begin a talk. In this area humor
must be used with caution. Sacrament meeting is to be a
spiritual meeting. We should avoid frivolity. In firesides, Sunday School, and other auxiliary meetings, appropriate humor
may be proper and welcome, but humor just to get a laugh is
never appropriate. Clever jokes or stories should be used to
introduce the subject of the talk, not strictly to amuse.

I know a cute story about a golfer who hit his ball into a
sandtrap just short of the green. His ball landed in an ant bed.
The golfer carefully surveyed the position of his ball, selected
the proper club, then stepped up to the ball. He gripped his club
and swung, completely missing the ball and scattering ants all
over the green. Disgusted at his performance, he again approached the ball, even more determined to chip it up out of the
sandtrap and onto the green. But once again he swung and
missed, and hundreds more ants were strewn all over the green.
One perceptive ant who had been watching the massacre of his
family and friends crawled up on top of the ball and shouted at
the top of his lungs: "Come on guys! We've got to get on the ball
if we want to be saved!"

This humorous story can be a delightful introduction to a
discussion of a saving gospel principle.

Here is another possible opener:

A man in a Cadillac pulled up to a red light. He didn't notice that the light had turned green. An impatient driver in a Volkswagen behind him started honking his horn, then leaned out his window and yelled to the man in the Cadillac: "Move the trashcan, pilgrim." The fellow in the Cadillac stepped out of his car and walked back to the Volkswagen. "I don't take that kind of guff from anybody," he said to the VW driver. The Volkswagen door opened and the man started to get out, and kept getting out, and kept getting out. When he was all the way out he was six feet five inches and weighed 260 pounds. The Cadillac driver, frightened by the other man's size, looked up at him and timidly said, "Don't you have some kind of guff I could take?"

If you are giving a talk and have some "guff that your listeners should take," you might want to begin with this clever story.

One final and appropriate use for humor is the situation in which the discussion or language gets a bit off-color. Don't be afraid to abruptly change the conversation with a bit of humor. You might want to tell this little anecdote. It's a true incident which happened at LDS Hospital some years ago.

Freddie, a little boy, had been operated on early in the morning. His mother sat with him during the long hours of the day. Finally at 7:00 P.M. she went to the head nurse and said, "I'm leaving now, but I would like you to check on Freddie every half hour."

The head nurse replied, "We'll check on him regularly, but we don't have time to check on him every half hour."

The concerned mother said, "I will not leave unless you promise to check on him every half hour."

The head nurse finally agreed. "You may leave," she said, "I promise to personally check on him every half hour."

At 7:30 P.M. the nurse made her way from the central station down to the very last room on the far end of the hall. She poked her head in the door and asked, "Freddie, how are you?"

"Just fine," he replied.

The nurse made several stops on her way back to the central station and finally got back to her station at 8:00, just in time to turn around and head back down the hall again. She put her head in the door and asked, "How are you doing, Freddie?"

"I'm doing okay," he said.

She turned around and returned to the central station. At

8:30 and 9:00 she made her check. Finally, discouraged from walking up and down the hall to Freddie's room and not getting her work done, she decided to use the intercom. She pushed the button to Freddie's room and asked, "Freddie, are you all right?" There wasn't a sound. She pushed the button a second time, "Are you okay?" Still nothing. "Freddie, speak to me. Are you all right down there?"

Then a very timid voice said, "Yes, Wall, what do you want?"

My young friends, strive to have a sweet, pleasant sense of humor. Good humor is the sanity of the soul. Use your sense of humor in the right time and in the right place. It can do much to bless your life — or, if improperly used, to seriously impair your relationships with others. Remember a little quotation from William Thakeray, "The best humor is that which contains the most humanity, that which is flavored throughout with tenderness and kindness." If you will remember this as you attempt to be clever and witty, you will add to your life a sense of humor which is both good and funny. That addition will be a significant building block in your character.

14

Yes, You Have Obligations

Are there some words you don't like to hear? Do you dislike being called a *teenager*? Do you react to the word *chastity*? Do you hate the word *work*? Or what about *math*? Perhaps you dislike the word *genealogy* — many people do because it evokes feelings of guilt, knowing it is something they need to do but may not want to do. Or what about the phrase "when I was your age"? You may even dislike hearing your own name when your mother or father calls it in that certain tone of voice which means: "Come here! I want to talk to you!"

Words aren't simply words any more. Over the years many words have come to acquire either emotional connotations or changed meanings, or sometimes both. The word *promiscuous*, for example, has come to be associated almost entirely with indiscriminate sexual behavior. But the word actually has a much broader definition, meaning miscellaneous, assorted, varied.

What do you feel when you hear the word *duty*? *Duty* is a word that carries both a strong emotional reaction as well as a slight modern change in meaning. People have come to associate *duty* with something unpleasant that's done against one's will. But duty is not a harsh word, and after reading this chapter I hope you will think of it as a noble word representing an equally noble concept.

Then just what is duty? I believe that duty is spontaneous performance when character is so trained. Let me illustrate with a story from a book which has probably influenced my life more than any other book short of the scriptures. That book is *Les Miserables* by Victor Hugo.

Jean Valjean, the central figure in the book, is persecuted by police because as a youth he stole a loaf of bread for some starving children. Even after serving time in the galleys at Toulon he is pursued by vindictive police officers, and to escape them he has changed his identity to Monsieur Madeleine. As Monsieur Madeleine he goes about performing good deeds as silently as evil ones are usually performed. In one incident in the book Monsieur Madeleine is walking alone one morning down an unpaved street when he hears a man shouting and sees a crowd gathering. As he approaches he sees that an accident has occurred and old Father Fauchelevent has fallen under his cart.

Father Fauchelevent and Monsieur Madeleine are not particularly good friends. Father Fauchelevent is jealous of Monsieur Madeleine, for he has watched Monsieur Madeleine grow rich while his own business has sadly declined until he is now a peddler with a horse and cart.

In the accident the horse has broken his thighs and cannot stir. The old man is caught between the wheels of the cart, which is heavily loaded. He has fallen so that the entire weight rests upon his chest. He cries out for assistance. Someone has gone for a jack but is not expected to return for at least fifteen minutes. It rained the night before, the street is soft, and the cart is sinking deeper and deeper every moment. In less than five minutes the old man's ribs will be crushed.

Monsieur Madeleine, realizing the urgency of the situation, shouts: "Listen, there is room enough still under the wagon for a man to crawl in, and lift it with his back. In half a minute we will have the poor man out. Is there nobody here who has strength and courage? Five louis d'ors for him!" But nobody stirs. Monsieur Madeleine raises the figure to ten louis, then twenty, and still no one responds.

A police officer in the crowd says: "Monsieur Madeleine, I

have known but one man capable of doing what you call for. He was a convict. In the galleys at Toulon." Madeleine turns pale.

Meanwhile the cart is slowly settling down. Father Fauchelevent screams with fright: "I am dying! My ribs are breaking!" Madeleine can no longer stand by and watch this man suffer. In a totally selfless act and heedless of the danger of disclosing his identity, he falls on his knees and climbs under the wagon.

Father Fauchelevent and the crowd call to Monsieur Madeleine to come out from under the cart, but Madeleine does not answer. The wheels are still sinking in the soft dirt and it has now become impossible for Monsieur Madeleine to free himself. Then all at once the cart starts to move, the wheels come half way out of the ruts, and a smothered voice beneath calls for help. The crowd rushes to Madeleine's aid. The devotion of one man has given strength and courage to all, and the old man's life is spared.

What was it that motivated Monsieur Madeleine to do this courageous act? Was it for self-aggrandizement? No. Was it out of devotion for the old man? Not especially. I believe it was duty — spontaneous performance when character is so trained. Jean Valjean, Monsieur Madeleine, had so patterned his life that to do otherwise would have been against his true self.

How do we develop this type of duty-bound character? First, we start by doing those things we know we ought to do, whether or not we particularly want to do them. There are many activities in your life which may fall under this category — like doing your homework, going home teaching, cleaning your room, collecting fast offerings, attending youth committee meetings, the list could go on and on. Sometimes it takes great discipline to perform these obligations. But duty and discipline always go hand in hand. Unfortunately discipline is becoming a difficult lesson to teach youth today. We live in a pleasure-oriented society and many young people are raised with the philosophy that they don't have to do anything they don't want to do. But this simply isn't true. Unless you want to go through life without ever really accomplishing anything, you must discipline yourself. It is good training to make yourself do at least one thing every day that you do not like to do. As I have discussed in chapter 9 on attitude, you will find that in time you will like to do the things you thought you didn't like to do. Remember the statement, "No pain, no gain." For example, if you don't discipline yourself to sit and practice a musical instrument for an hour a day, can you ever gain proficiency in playing that instrument? If you constantly watch television instead of reading worthwhile literature, can you expect to learn to like to read, to become efficient at it, and to become a knowledgeable person? If you don't discipline yourself to struggle through a math problem, regardless of how difficult it may be, can you ever expect to know the thrill of accomplishment and achieve good grades?

These areas are ones in which you have a duty only to yourself; you are the one who merits the direct gain or loss from the discipline and effort extended. But what about the areas in which you have a duty to others? Then how important is it that you discipline yourself to do your responsibility?

A classic story is told by Willard R. Smith who was a deacon in Salt Lake City in pioneer days:

"As a deacon, I was assigned to gather the 'fast' on our block. A bewhiskered, beyond-middle-aged gentleman, Brother Peter Reid, was the supervisor, and it was his responsibility to see that the fast offerings were gathered and distributed to the needy on our block. He would call at our home every Friday, tell me that the little 'express wagon' was dusted and oiled, ready for the job.

"I was to visit every home on the block, both members and non-members alike, and give them the opportunity to give something for the benefit of the poor. One home would give a large lump of coal, another some wood, another a scoop of flour, a bottle of fruit, a cup of sugar, a slab of bacon, and so forth. I would have to make several trips to Brother Reid's home with an overloaded red express wagon before the job was complete. The non-members seemed to be just as generous as the members.

"On a particular Saturday our football team had scheduled a game and I was eager to play. I knew it was my duty to gather the 'fast' and it would be wrong if I failed, but I wanted more than anything else to play that game. I chose pleasure over duty, and played football. To this day I bear a scar on my face as a result.

"Early the next morning Brother Reid knocked on our back door and asked for me. I was conscience stricken — I wanted to run and hide — but I faced him, head down. All he said was: 'Willard, do you have time to take a little walk with me?'

"It was a cold fall day.

"I went with him, first to a little frame court near the corner of First North and Third West streets. He gently rapped on one of the doors and a poor little thin lady answered the door.

"She said: 'Brother Reid, we didn't get our food yesterday and we haven't a thing in the house to eat.'

"Brother Reid said: 'I'm sorry, sister, but I'm sure we'll have something for you before the close of the day.'

"We went to another door near the upper end of the court. In response to our knock a voice called for us to come in.

"We entered to find an aged man and his wife in bed. He said: 'Brother Reid, we are without coal, and we have to stay in bed to keep warm.'

"In another part of the court we were greeted by a little mother with her small children huddled together. The baby was crying and the other children had tear-stained faces.

"That was enough! As we parted Brother Reid said gently, 'Willard, whenever anybody fails to do his duty, someone suffers.'

"I was about to cry — overwhelmed by my appalling neglect of duty. He laid his hand on my shoulder and left. Those people had their food and coal early that afternoon — and I learned a most valuable lesson." (*Program Outline for Teaching Observance of the Law of the Fast*, 1965, pages 19-20.)

The second step in developing a duty-bound character is to avoid making excuses for ourselves. We must do our duty regardless of the personal inconveniences or costs involved. Lynn Fluckiger in his book *Dynamic Leadership* makes this statement about excuses:

"Any excuse for nonperformance, however valid, softens the character. It is a sedative against one's own conscience. When a man uses an excuse he attempts to convince both himself and others that unsatisfactory is somehow acceptable. . . .

"To use an excuse is a habit. We cannot have both the performance habit *and* the excuse habit. We all have a supply of excuses. The more we use them the lower become our standards, the poorer our performance. The better we perform, the less plausible our excuses become.

"Next time you want to defend your slothfulness, say instead (at least to yourself): 'No excuse.' Notice the startling effect this will have on your self-respect. You will have recognized your failure. You will have been honest with yourself. You will be a step closer to the performance habit. You will be a better man." (W. Lynn Fluckiger, *Dynamic Leadership*, Deseret Book Company, 1962, pages 53-54.)

I once met a stake president who told me about a remarkable young man who would not let excuses interfere with the performance of his duties. This stake president was a medical doctor, and one day at work he shared the gospel with one of his patients. The lady seemed interested and agreed to see the missionaries. The stake president made the necessary arrangements, but for some reason the woman was not visited.

About six weeks later she returned to the stake president's professional office. At the conclusion of her appointment she asked, "I thought you were going to send two young men to see me?"

The stake president was embarrassed and apologized for the elders' oversight, then promised her that two missionaries would be out to see her immediately. He then contacted two other elders whom he knew would not fail to call upon this woman.

One of these elders had a crippled foot, which made it difficult for him to walk. When the stake president called, this young man promised that he and his companion would see this lady right away. After hanging up the phone, the elder remembered that his bicycle had been stolen and that he was therefore without transportation. But he had already made the commitment and he did not make excuses for nonperformance. So this wonderful young elder and his companion walked eight miles to give this woman the first discussion, then they walked the eight miles home. Even then his duty was not fulfilled. The woman wanted to hear the other discussions, so for three weeks he and his companion walked those eight miles to her home to give her the missionary lessons. Eventually she was baptized.

That young man knew what it meant to be duty-bound.

But as important as duty is, it is only the median point on a continuum ranging from nonperformance on one end to the highest motivation, love, on the other. In other words, on a scale of 0 to 10, duty would be only half way — 5. But duty is the starting point toward the higher level. Through conscientiously performing our duty we climb the scale from 5 to 6, 6 to 7, and so on.

For example, I know a young priesthood holder who was given the responsibility of home teaching with an older gentleman in his ward. He went because he sensed that it was his duty, though he would rather have been playing basketball, working in his dad's shop, or even doing his homework. He thought that the visits were a waste of time and that the conversations with the families were trivial.

Then one day the father of one of the families they home taught mentioned that his son, who was close to the same age as this young priesthood holder, was failing school. He was frequently staying out late and had started associating with an undesirable crowd. Suddenly the young home teacher had a personal interest in this family. He had noticed that this boy had frequently been absent from the English class which they took together. He felt a strong desire to become this boy's friend, to help steer him away from his undesirable associates, and to help him with his English assignments.

And that is exactly what this young home teacher did. Although his efforts at first were met with skepticism and mistrust, in time he was successful in bringing this boy back into activity at school and at church.

The interesting point of this story is not the change which occurred in the wayward boy but that in the young priesthood holder. He was actually anxious to visit the father of his friend and to report on his progress. Instead of the usual one visit toward the end of the month, he visited often, for he had learned to genuinely care about this boy and his family. What had started on level 5, duty, had progressed to level 6 or 7 or 8 as this young priesthood holder learned the joy and satisfaction that come from loving and serving others.

What things have others done for you out of duty? Most service in the Church is first rendered out of duty. It is duty which unites your quorum or class presidency each week when they might rather be skiing or bicycling. No doubt your advisor would sometimes prefer being home with his or her family than going on some of your class outings. And your bishop would sometimes like to sleep in on a Sunday morning but never can because the pressures of the day require that he be at the church early to start. Duty gets him out of bed. Each of these people, and many others in your life, has accepted a responsibility, and duty prompts him to action. Through faithful performance of that obligation they have progressed along the continuum; acts of duty become acts of love.

The Savior knew that he would have to endure tremendous agony to atone for our sins. And he knew something of the excruciating pain of crucifixion. Yet in the preexistence he had committed himself to the Father that he would be our redeemer. He expressed his sense of this commitment in the Garden of Gethsemane when he prayed, "O my Father, if it be possible, let this cup pass from me: *nevertheless not as I wilt, but as thou wilt."* (Matthew 26:39. Italics added.) And yet even as the Savior underwent this terrible agony he did not do it solely out of duty but also out of love. For we know that "God so *loved* the world, that he gave his only begotten Son . . ." (John 3:16, italic added), and the Son was like the Father. Thus he also *loved.*

On the duty scale, however, there is actually one level higher than love. That level — shall we call it level 15? — is joy. Joyful service is the ultimate achievement. It is higher than doing our duty because it is our obligation. It is even higher than doing our duty because we are motivated by love. But from this love we can learn to serve *joyfully.* The Savior did the Father's will joyfully. And I believe that those who merit a place with him in his Father's kingdom will find that there is no particular sense of duty there, but only joyful, loving service.

Regardless of where you may be today on the duty scale, accept and perform your obligations faithfully and with a happy heart. If you have responsibilities that you don't particularly enjoy, try changing your attitude about them, for your attitude can make the difference between a chore and a challenge, a drudgery and a delight.

I have always had great respect for the General Authorities of the Church. Since I was called to associate with these outstanding men I have studied their lives so that I might incorporate into my own their sterling qualities. I have found one distinguishing characteristic which they all possess. That quality is dependability. They are duty-bound. And how they have grown from incorporating this building tool into their lives!

Accepting responsibility is an essential building block. You too will grow immeasurably from it. Yes, you have obligations. And aren't you glad of it!

15

The Strength of Ten

If you have taken biology you undoubtedly have had to dissect a frog. From what I hear, formaldehyde frogs are a thing of the past. The idea these days is to catch one of the slippery, squirmy live ones, then insert a straight pin through its brain. The pin paralyzes the frog but does not kill it, allowing you to open its chest and observe the operation of its internal organs.

After a friend of mine had had this experience in school, he described in great detail how the tiny heart, smaller than the nail of your little finger, pumped blood through the miniature arteries and veins. He was fascinated by the steady, never-ceasing operation of the little red muscle, around which the frog's very existence revolved.

Human existence too is dependent upon the heart. But besides being the hub of our physical well-being, the heart has also come to represent the center of many emotions. Think of all the adjectives and phrases which are ascribed to the heart — heartfelt, bighearted, heartbroken, heartless, heartwarming, heartsick, good-hearted. . . . And there is one other heart expression which particularly comes to mind — purity of heart.

If the Lord were the observer looking inside us, what would he be most interested in viewing? Just as my friend had been most impressed with the frog's heart, I believe that the Lord would most want to observe our hearts. He would want to see if they are pure.

To be pure in heart is a most desirable quality. The Savior said, "Blessed are the pure in heart: for they shall see God." (Matthew 5:8.) To merit such a great reward, purity of heart must indeed be a noble virtue. But just exactly what does it mean?

In search of an answer I went to Elder Bruce R. McConkie's book *Mormon Doctrine*. His definition said in part that the pure in heart are those who are free from moral defilement or guilt. Let's dissect that definition and examine it more closely.

I have discussed the subject of morality in some detail in chapter 7, but because it is so important let me just say two additional things about it here. I would like to relate part of a message Elder Hartman Rector, Jr. gave on the subject in the October 1972 general conference.

Elder Rector said that when he was in the navy "flat hatting" was a very popular sport. "Flat hatting" was flying just as low and close to the treetops as possible. The danger of this sport, however, was that if the plane's engine should cough even once, the plane and pilot were in the trees.

Naturally the navy frowned on pilots who flew their planes into trees and thus expressly forbade "flat hatting." In order to prevent violating the navy commandment "Thou shalt not fly thine airplane in the trees," Elder Rector added an additional commandment of his own: "Thou shalt not fly thine airplane closer than 5,000 feet to the trees."

Elder Rector explained that additional commandments are sometimes necessary to help us obey God's laws. We have been commanded "Thou shalt not commit adultery," or fornication, in the case of unmarried people. In order to help you keep that commandment and avoid moral defilement, you need to establish a few additional commandments of your own. Elder Rector suggested these:

1. Never go into a house alone with one of the opposite sex.
2. Never, never enter a bedroom alone with one of the opposite sex.
3. Do not neck or pet.

4. Never park on a lonely road with just the two of you alone.

5. Do not read pornographic literature.

6. Do not attend R- or X-rated movies, and avoid drive-ins.

7. Do not spend time in drinking or gambling establishments.

These extra commandments will help keep you well away from the temptation and danger of immorality.

But looking once more at Elder McConkie's definition, it says "free of moral defilement *or guilt*." Those two additional words "or guilt" carry a beautiful message. That message is forgiveness. For if a person has transgressed the law of chastity, yet has a conviction of guilt and a desire to become pure in heart and receive forgiveness, he may do so through the beautiful principle of repentance. Elder McConkie explains: "To gain forgiveness through repentance a person must have a conviction of guilt, a godly sorrow for sin, and a contrite spirit. He must desire to be relieved of the burden of sin, have a fixed determination to forsake his evil ways, be willing to confess his sins, and forgive those who have trespassed against him. . . ." (Bruce R. McConkie, *Mormon Doctrine*, Bookcraft, 1966, page 630.)

Thus a sorrow for sin begins the process of repentance through which everyone has the opportunity to take an important step towards becoming pure in heart by being free of moral defilement or guilt.

To have purity of heart we must also have purity of thought. The scriptures tell us "For as he [a man] thinketh in his heart, so is he." (Proverbs 23:7.) What we think can have a profound effect on what we do. Our thoughts can either elevate our lives or destroy them.

I know of a young returned missionary who through associations at work became very friendly with a group of non-LDS youth who did not have the same standards as he. Nevertheless he frequently "partied" with them after work, claiming that he did not have to partake of their lifestyle to enjoy being with this friendly group who gave him such a release from the problems and pressures of his life. That first rationalization led to many others — to drink, drugs, and then immorality. Now his thoughts were totally impure, his peace of mind destroyed, and his heart laden with guilt. His thoughts had led to self-destructive acts which lost him his Church membership, his self-pride, and the respect of family and friends.

Meanwhile others who had served a mission at the same time as he had were happily pursuing the opposite path. With their thoughts under the calming and pleasant influence of the gospel, they pursued wholesome friendships, found worthy partners, married in the temple, and began to raise families which were and would continue to be a joy to their lives.

Each of us, then, can either allow his thoughts to overpower his desire to keep the commandments or, by thinking good and uplifting thoughts, help to make himself a more Christlike person. The choice is yours. If you desire purity of heart, don't let unclean, unwholesome thoughts linger in your mind. Immediately replace them with noble, uplifting ones. Elder Boyd K. Packer suggested that one way we can do this is by memorizing the words to a favorite hymn. Use this hymn as an "emergency channel" — a place for your thoughts to go. He said: "As the words [to the hymn] form in your thoughts, the unworthy ones will slip shamefully away. It will change the whole mood on the stage of your mind. Because it is unlifting and clean, the baser thoughts will disappear. For while virtue, by choice, *will not* associate with filth, evil *cannot* tolerate the presence of light."

In addition to shoving out unwholesome thoughts, we need to avoid unkind ones. Sometimes it is difficult to avoid dwelling on someone else's peculiarities. Sometimes we think unkind things about someone because it makes us feel superior. But if we seek to pattern our lives after the Savior and have purity of heart, we must "let virtue garnish our thoughts unceasingly."

Elder McConkie's definition of purity of heart also says that the pure in heart are those who have "bridled their passions, put off the natural man and become saints through the atonement." Who is the natural man? I'm afraid most of us are. A natural man is one who responds to natural impulses rather than spiritual ones. Let me illustrate with a story told by Leland Anderson.

"In my home town was a large pea factory. Peas were never picked in the patch; they were cut in the vine like hay, and loaded — green vines and all — on a hay wagon. A relatively small forkful could seem like a load of lead.

"One morning as I was mowing some alfalfa, the fieldman from the factory came to me and said, 'Your pea patch is ready right now to be harvested.' This is a crucial point — a few hours of too much sunshine turns peas in a pod from first-class to hard tack. Much value of the crop is lost if it is not cut on time.

"I moved my team and hay-cutting equipment to the five-acre pea patch and in a short time had cut all the hayrack would hold; in fact, it was all my small team could pull. With some effort and the help of a switch, I managed to get the team to pull the load to the hardened field road. Then we proceeded toward the factory a mile away. However, I had forgotten all about the old field ditch, full of water, which my team had to cross. Would I ever make it?

"I soon discovered the answer. Approaching the ditch, I first gave the team a much-needed rest. Then, with positive urging, they shot across the ditch — but the front wheels hit the mud and sank up to the hub!

"The only solution was for me to unload all the peas on the ground, pull the empty wagon across, and then proceed to carry the peas and replace them upon the wagon. The very thought made me tired. If only another team and wagon would appear on the scene — maybe two teams could pull me out!

"Then up the road I could see an outfit coming in my direction. Help was in sight. As the wagon came closer, however, my heart sank. It was my neighbor who lived down the road and who did not help anyone. He didn't have to — he was rich in worldly goods.

"As he pulled up beside me, he stopped his outfit and smilingly said, 'So, you're stuck, are you, Lee?' I was surprised he knew my name. He had never talked to me before. I replied that my load was too big for my small team. His smile grew larger as he said, 'Well, good luck to you,' and away he went down the lane.

"Never was I so angry! What I called him cannot be printed — I even spoke in Danish so my team couldn't understand! For the moment I reappraised the law of Moses. I looked up into the sky and said, 'Oh, Father, give me the chance to meet him on the desert some time, choking for a good drink of water. Let me have a barrel of water in my truck so I can pour it out onto the sand and tell him to scratch.'

"Somehow I managed to get to the factory. I succeeded in

getting all of my peas harvested in time, and though my feelings were still on edge they had mellowed somewhat.

"Evil seldom requires a down payment; it's like installment buying. My hope — and my day — finally arrived. A few days later, while proceeding to my farm, as I approached this roadblock to my farming efforts, the ditch, I nearly choked with happiness. I found my unobliging neighbor stuck in the same ditch with a load of peas! . . .

"As I pulled up beside my brother, I stopped and repeated to him his own words: 'So you're stuck, are you, brother?' My neighbor responded that he could not proceed without help. I did not wait longer. I jumped off my wagon, took from it a long chain, and secured it properly onto the end of his wagon tongue. Then the two teams put their shoulders to the wheel and in short order they were all standing on dry ground.

"In deep embarrassment, my neighbor said, 'Thanks, Lee. I appreciate your kindness.' Then he added, 'How much do I owe you?'

"My reply was not altogether honest. 'I enjoyed helping you out of that ditch,' I said.

"We both went on our way rejoicing. I could hardly hold my team — they seemed to want to trot. And I caught myself whistling and singing 'Come, Come Ye Saints.'

"A couple of days later I found a new bridge over the ditch. I smiled as I learned who had obliged all the north field farmers with this needed contribution.

"Two weeks later, while cutting more hay one day, I noticed a man coming down through my field. It was my neighbor. 'Let your team have a break, while we settle the problems of the world,' he said. So we visited for a few minutes. Then, as he started to leave, he looked squarely at me and, in halting phrases, apologized for leaving me in the ditch." (Leland E. Anderson, "Don't Dam Your Spiritual Garden," *Stories of Power and Purpose*, Bookcraft, 1974, pages 6-9.)

Brother Anderson had bridled his passions by restraining his desire to retaliate. The impulse to strike back, to get even, is but one of many natural impulses. But instead Brother Anderson responded to the higher, more spiritual impulse to turn the other cheek, to agree with his adversary, to love his neighbor.

In King Benjamin's discourse he tells us that the natural man is an enemy to God and that we must put off the natural man and become as a child, "submissive, meek, humble, patient, full of love. . . ." (Mosiah 3:19.)

Are there areas in your life in which you need to "bridle your passions" and control the natural instinct? Perhaps your temper occasionally needs checking. Is it easy to gossip a bit about someone? Is it a natural instinct to be less than totally honest, especially when your own position is questioned? Or are your passions more physical? Does your appetite for food need restraining? Or do you have a passion for sleep? Or maybe your passion is new clothes, skiing, television, cars, or any of a hundred other things which may be all right in moderation but may become a passion when used in excess. We must overcome these passions and bridle our natural impulses if we want to become saints.

The scriptures are replete with admonitions to become pure in heart. "And I give unto you . . . a commandment that you assemble yourselves together, and organize yourselves, and prepare yourselves, and sanctify yourselves; yea, purify your hearts. . . ." (D&C 88:74.) We are also told in the scriptures that purity of hearts is an attainable goal. In Helaman we read that many of the Nephites did "wax stronger and stronger in their humility, and firmer and firmer in the faith of Christ . . . even to the purifying and the sanctification of their hearts." (Helaman 3:35.) The people of Enoch attained such a high degree of perfection and purity that the Lord himself dwelt with them and in time the entire city was "taken up into heaven." (Moses 7:16-21.)

But there are also intermediate rewards which come to us as we work on this important principle. One of these is mental and physical strength. In the Book of Mormon we learn of the two thousand young warriors who were called the sons of Helaman. These noble young men had been told by their mothers that if they did not doubt the Lord, he would protect them. And because they lived righteously the Lord blessed them with unusual physical strength and watched over them in battle. Following a particularly vicious battle with the Lamanites, Helaman counted his young men and found that not one had been killed. He wrote:

"And now it came to pass that when they [the Lamanites] had surrendered themselves up unto us, behold, I numbered those young men who had fought with me, fearing lest there were many of them slain. But behold, to my great joy, there was not one soul of them fallen to the earth; yea, and they had fought as if with the strength of God; yea, never were men known to have fought with such miraculous strength. . . ." (Alma 56:55-56.)

Alfred Tennyson, an English poet who lived during the nineteenth century, wrote a poem entitled "Sir Galahad." Sir Galahad was the noblest knight of the Round Table in the legends of King Arthur. Two of his lines in the poem have become famous because of their beautiful message: "My strength is as the strength of ten,/Because my heart is pure."

You too will come to realize great mental and physical strength as you purify your heart. Keep the commandments. Repent of your transgressions. Purify your thoughts. Bridle your passions. Then when the day comes that your life is dissected and examined, the Lord will look into your heart and find it as pure and clear as crystal.

16

It Never
Fails

Despite the mass production of the modern world, some hand
crafts remain. There are, for example, still schools that train
students in the art of crafting handmade violins. One thing the
students learn is the importance of using only wood which has
been properly seasoned. In fact, the wood must age from twelve
to fifteen years before it will impart to the violin the proper
resonance.

The students in the violin-making school learn to know
intimately each piece of aged wood. They know its density and
hence its vibrating ability. Some pieces of wood will be carefully
hand carved into a smooth soundboard, others into an intricate
scroll, a finger-board, a bridge, and so on. Once the pieces have
been skillfully fashioned and properly assembled, the violin
undergoes a varnishing process which takes from three to four
months. Each coat of varnish is meticulously hand-rubbed until
the final instrument is as beautiful in appearance as it is in
function.

Between 150 and 200 hours of hand labor, in addition to the
preliminary twelve to fifteen years of aging, are required to
fashion a flawless violin. Yet even as perfect as these in-

struments are when completed, they will never produce beautiful music unless they have one final, essential element — strings.

There is a parallel between these carefully fashioned violins and our lives. We can have the very best materials available and spend hours, months, years crafting our lives, acquiring the virtues of honesty, integrity, humility, purity, and so on, but we can fail to sing a sweet song without one essential element. That element, which is as important to our exaltation as strings are to the utility of the violin, is *charity*.

Mormon wrote, "Wherefore, my beloved brethren, if ye have not charity, ye are nothing, for charity never faileth." (Moroni 7:46.) Above all the attributes of godliness and perfection which we are capable of acquiring, charity is the one we should most ardently desire. Moroni tells us, "Except ye have charity ye can in nowise be saved in the kingdom of God." (Moroni 10:21.)

What is charity? Some say it is a synonym for love, but charity is more than love. Charity is everlasting love, perfect love, a love for everyone, the pure love of Christ which endures forever. It is love so centered in righteousness that he who possesses charity has no aim or desire except for the eternal welfare of his own soul and the souls around him.

Jesus Christ is our most perfect example of charity. His sole purpose was to come to earth and put into operation the plan of redemption, salvation, and exaltation. Through his pure love for us we are given the gift of immortality and the potential of exaltation. In the Book of Ether is recorded these words of Moroni unto the Lord: "And again, I remember that thou hast loved the world, even unto the laying down of thy life for the world, that thou mightest take it again to prepare a place for the children of men. And now I know that this love which thou hast had for the children of men is charity; wherefore, except men shall have charity they cannot inherit that place which thou hast prepared in the mansions of thy Father." (Ether 12:33-34.)

As we attempt to emulate the example given us by our Savior, we must realize that charity is not something we can hastily acquire. The Savior spent thirty years preparing himself for his mission. While every kindness we bestow is a step in the right direction, an occasional act of charity on our part will not make us a charitable person and merit us a place in our Father's kingdom. It requires a lifetime of effort.

A young girl once said to her mother, after a lovely white-haired visitor had left their home, "If I could be as lovable, beautiful and sweet as that woman, I wouldn't mind growing old." The discerning mother replied: "If you want to be that kind of person in your old age you had best begin now. She does not impress me as being a piece of work that was done in a hurry." Neither is acquiring the virtue of charity a piece of work that can be done in a hurry.

How do we become charitable? How do we learn to truly love one another? Merely saying "I love you" is not enough. Christ demonstrated his love for his disciples not by mere words alone but through his actions. He served them. And this too is the way we can learn to have charity — by serving one another.

Some years ago when I was a seminary teacher in Boise, Idaho, the students in my seminary class took a good step toward becoming charitable people. They decided to sub for Santa at Christmas. They selected a family with eight children who resided in our stake and were semi-active in the Church. The family was poor, and the class felt certain that they would not have a Christmas without our help.

The class members first collected suits, shirts, skirts and blouses which were still in good condition. Then they decided to raise $75 with which to buy new toys for the children and food for a Christmas dinner. The students frugally saved their money; and a week before school was to let out for the holidays they had approximately $65, which they had stored in a jar in our seminary cupboard at the ward. But when they went to the cupboard that day to count the funds at their disposal, they discovered that the jar was gone. Someone had stolen it. The students were dismayed. They could not believe that anyone would steal that money. I asked the class president, "What will you do now?" "We will start all over again and raise the money," he said.

Then I saw a miracle take place. These choice young people, who had been going without lunch once or twice a week to raise the money, now decided to go without lunch every day. How hard they worked to earn money that last week! By the end of that week, when school was ready to let out for the holidays, they had raised $73.

The class met at 3:00 P.M. on Christmas Eve. The clothes they had donated and the toys they had purchased were wrapped and tagged. The students had bought a turkey for the family's Christmas dinner. It was placed in one of several food boxes, then loaded on a delivery truck with all the other Christmas packages.

One of the students had volunteered her father to be Santa Claus. Led by jolly old St. Nick and his truck of goodies, we drove as a group across town to the area where the needy family lived. The family's home was down a long, dark, dirt road. As we approached the home we could see the mother and two children standing on the back porch. The woman held her hands up to shadow her eyes from the porch light and peered out into the darkness. I could see she was concerned over our unexpected arrival, so I yelled: "Don't be afraid. It's Santa Claus!" Santa jumped out of the car and headed across the lawn. His bells were ringing as he shouted, "Ho, ho, ho!" One of the little boys standing by his mother cried out: "It's him! It's really him! It's Santa Claus!"

Santa went right into the house and into the living room. The rest of the family was gathered around a scrawny little tree with a few decorations on it. Half a box of oranges was under the tree, nothing more. While Santa was inside, the students began to unload the gifts onto the back porch. We each took two or three arm-loads. One of the younger children heard us and came to watch us fill their large screened-in back porch with gifts. He signaled to his brothers and sisters, and soon all the children were lined up watching Santa's helpers deliver the gifts and food. When the gifts were unloaded we returned to the cars and waited for Santa Claus. After he had bid the family "Merry Christmas," he hopped in the car and we all drove back to the ward in silence.

Back at the church we all stood on the lawn and talked about the experience. The class president expressed the feelings of us all: "When that little kid stood on the back porch and said: 'It's him! It's really him! It's Santa Claus!' I had a feeling I've never had before in my life." The tears came to his eyes and he could not say any more. We all felt the same way. We gathered together and offered a prayer, then adjourned to our own homes for Christmas Eve with our families.

The seminary students were richly blessed for their love and compassion. But what of the family who could not afford to give? Were they less blessed? No. Certainly they were blessed with the gifts of toys and food, but they were also blessed for not offending those who gave. They were charitable receivers. The father did not let false pride spoil the experience for the givers. The family welcomed the Christmas gifts with such child-like excitement and uncontained joy that it was a happy experience for all. Both the givers and the receivers learned a great lesson in charity that year.

Just after I was made a General Authority I moved with my family into the Crescent-Draper area. As we entered the church building for the first time, we saw a huge cardboard thermometer in the lobby with a goal at the top of $74,000. Money was being raised for a new Crescent Second Ward building and stake center, and everyone was asked to contribute to help the mercury in the thermometer hit the $74,000 goal.

Christmastime was approaching, and my wife and I decided that we needed to hold a special family home evening to determine as a family how we could best allocate the Christmas funds and still meet our building assessment. We decided to have each family member write down what he wanted for Christmas. At family home evening each child passed in a little note with his Christmas requests. I read them one by one, and then I came to Joe's. His note was very special. He wrote: "Dear Dad — Please give all of my Christmas to the building fund. Thank you for your cooperation. Do with my Christmas as you may. Love, Joe." After family home evening I asked Joe, "Are you serious?" He said, "Yes, I really am."

The following week I gave the bishop a check for the amount of money my wife and I had planned to spend for Joe's Christmas. I asked the bishop to write out a receipt in Joe Featherstone's name showing his donation to the fund.

As my wife and I put out the toys for the family on Christmas Eve, I slipped this receipt into Joe's stocking, along with an orange, some candy, and a few little things. That was all Joe would receive from Santa Claus that Christmas. I could hardly sleep that night, wondering if I had done the right thing.

On Christmas morning I was especially anxious to see how Joe would react. He went over to his chair; nothing was there from Santa Claus. He reached in his stocking and pulled out the little slip of paper, then got a bit teary-eyed. But I still wasn't sure exactly how he felt. Several hours later some of Joe's friends came by to see what Joe had received for Christmas. He said that he had received a slip of paper 2½ inches wide and 5 inches long. "Wasn't much of a Christmas was it, Joe?" they said. But Joe replied, "It was the best Christmas I have ever had."

I too believe that that Christmas was Joe's best, for when we are more concerned about someone else, or in this case the Lord's cause, than ourselves, we are most Christlike. I am sure Joe felt closer to the Savior that year than any other Christmas in his life. That year Joe learned the meaning of charity. What a disservice I would have rendered had I not granted Joe his wish!

We often hear of charity in connection with Christmas, as that season brings out the Christlike attributes in each of us. But charity is something we must come to possess year-round. It is a gift of the Spirit which we can receive through earnest prayer. Mormon wrote, "Wherefore, my beloved brethren, pray unto the Father with all the energy of heart, that ye may be filled with this love, which he hath bestowed upon all who are true followers of his Son, Jesus Christ." (Moroni 7:48.)

Our ability to be charitable does not depend upon our material resources. It does not matter how much we have to give. The Lord is concerned with our willingness to give. Recall the experience of our Savior as he stood and watched people casting money into the treasury. There were many that were rich and cast in large sums. Then there came a certain poor widow who threw in two mites. A mite was the seventh part of one piece of their brass money. The Savior called his disciples to him and said to them: "Verily I say unto you, That this poor widow hath cast more in, than all they which have cast into the treasury. For all they did cast in of their abundance; but she of her want did cast in all that she had, even all her living." (Matthew 12:43-44.)

But is material giving enough to acquire charity? The apostle Paul says no. "And though I bestow all my goods to feed the poor, and though I give my body to be burned, and have not charity, it profiteth me nothing." (1 Corinthians 13:1.)

Then what more is required of us? Paul continues, "Charity suffereth long and is kind." To possess the perfect love which Jesus demonstrated we must "suffer long," or in other words, we must have patience, and we must be gentle. "Charity envieth not;" we must not covet or envy that which another possesses. "Charity vaunteth not itself, is not puffed up." To vaunt means to make a vain display of one's own worth or attainments. To be puffed up is to be proud or conceited. These are not qualities of a person possessed of charity. Humility is indispensable to charity.

The scripture continues to tell us that charity "doth not behave itself unseemly." If we indulge in undignified behavior and go against established standards of good conduct and taste, we are behaving unseemly. This is not charity.

Charity "seeketh not her own." One meaning of this seems to be that the charitable person will sometimes allow himself to be imposed upon. I know of a sweet young woman whose husband selfishly spent his pay check on his own frivolous entertainment. He continually bought new cars, boats, and sporting equipment and scarcely provided his wife and family with sufficient food and clothing. Many women in similar circumstances would have "gone home to mother," but this sweet sister suffered in silence and endured. Finally, after many years and much prayer on her part, and through the help of the bishop, the situation changed. Her husband recognized his selfishness and immaturity and mended his ways. A marriage which could easily have ended in divorce was saved because this sister possessed charity and "sought not her own."

Charity "is not easily provoked." One of the greatest personality traits a person can possess is the ability to control his temper. When we give in to the rise of passion and temper we often "behave unseemly."

Charity "thinketh no evil." Can you imagine the President of the Church or the Savior thinking evil, vile thoughts? Certainly not. He who possesses charity has perfect control over his thoughts. The next verse, "Rejoiceth not in iniquity, but rejoiceth in the truth," goes hand in hand with thinking no evil. Sinful deeds first begin as sinful thoughts. To possess charity we must instead rejoice in that which is beautiful and true. (1 Corinthians 13:4-6.)

By now you are probably thinking, "This all sounds very noble, but surely it's virtually an impossible task." Not so. We would not be commanded, "Be ye therefore perfect, even as your Father which is in heaven is perfect," if it were not an attainable goal. It is however a *lifetime* goal. We cannot hope to accomplish it in a week, or a month, or even a year. But as we devote ourselves to the service of others and thus to the service of our Heavenly Father, we will come to possess this perfect, everlasting love.

One of the most beautiful stories of true Christlike, unselfish love is the story of Abram and Zimri. These two men were brothers. Abram had a wife and seven sons; Zimri had no family. Every day, year after year, they worked side by side in the fields. At harvest time they equally divided the bounties; Abram took half and Zimri took half.

One night after the harvest had been gathered, Abram sat in his home with his wife and seven sons and thought: "It isn't right. I have a wife and seven sons to give me joy; Zimri has neither wife nor children. It isn't fair that we should share alike. I will go out and take from my harvest a third of the sheaves and place it on Zimri's harvest. We should not share alike, for I am so greatly blessed." So Abram went out and took a generous third of the sheaves from his harvest and placed it on Zimri's pile.

That same night Zimri sat in his home and thought: "It isn't right that we should share alike. My brother Abram has seven sons and a wife to feed, whereas I am all alone. He needs more than I do. I will go out and take a generous third of my harvest and place it on Abram's harvest." So Zimri stealthily crept out into the night, took from his harvest a third of the sheaves, and placed it on Abram's harvest.

The next morning each of the brothers noticed that his pile was unchanged; the harvest remained equally divided. Both thought deeply about this matter, but not one word was said between them about the harvest. That night again they retired to their homes. Once again after dark Abram went out into his fields and took a third of the sheaves from his harvest and placed it on Zimri's harvest. Then he went back into the darkness where he could wait and watch. Soon he saw a figure in the darkness coming towards the harvest. He watched as Zimri removed a third of the sheaves of his harvest and placed it on Abram's. Abram then came forth from hiding and fell upon his brother and embraced him. Neither could speak because their joy was full.

Such an example of unselfish love is the kind of love we must come to possess toward all men if we are to possess true charity. So let's start now to give of ourselves. Let's become like the perfectly crafted handmade violins, when they are properly strung and tuned. We shouldn't want to be like ordinary manufactured violins. The components of those violins are routinely machine-cut from a standard pattern. Little regard is paid to the density and hence the tonal capacity of the wood. The pieces are quickly assembled. The finished products are good, but far from superior. Experienced handcraftsmen say the chances of producing a truly superior-quality violin from this manufacturing process are one in one thousand.

If we do not skillfully and carefully craft our lives and include in them the most important of all Christian virtues, charity, the chances of our returning to our Heavenly Father are less than one in one thousand. Let's not be ordinary violins. Let's start today by serving one another, then over the years we will age and mellow into perfect instruments of our Heavenly Father.

17

The King Is
Expecting You

Well, here you are starting the last chapter of the book. Each chapter has tried to equip you with a valuable tool to help you begin to shape your block of wood. Each tool which I have discussed is important in building your destiny. But there is one tool which will smooth and polish and perfect your block of wood more than any other. Like sandpaper to your do-it-yourself project, that tool is spirituality.

Many years ago Elder Bruce R. McConkie and I were assigned to a stake conference. At that conference Elder McConkie made a statement which I have thought about every day since. He said, "No other talent exceeds spirituality." I believe it is equally true that "no other tool exceeds spirituality." I believe this because, while all the other tools are invaluable in building your destiny, no other tool can get you closer to our Father in heaven than spirituality.

How do you gain spirituality? First, pray. Prayer is a private interview with the Father of our spirits. It is intense conversation in which we have the opportunity both to acknowledge his blessings to us and to ask for his help with our daily problems. But sometimes we get too caught up in asking and forget to acknowledge; or we become so impressed with our own importance that we forget to pray altogether. We know from the scriptures that the Lord is displeased when we do not remember to pray. While the people of Jared were dwelling in tents on the seashore in the wilderness prior to coming to the Promised Land, they began to forget the Lord. The Lord chastised the brother of Jared, perhaps because he had ceased to pray with the fervor and frequency with which he had prayed in the past. The Book of Mormon account tells us: "And it came to pass at the end of four years that the Lord came again unto the brother of Jared, and stood in a cloud and talked with him. And for the space of three hours did the Lord talk with the brother of Jared, and chastened him because he remembered not to call upon the name of the Lord." (Ether 2:14.)

Make prayer a constant and vital part of your life. Your spirit can come to depend on the sustenance and strength it receives from the Lord through prayer just as much as your physical body depends on the sustenance and strength it derives from food. I learned this many years ago when I was a deacon.

On the Sunday prior to Thanksgiving a member of the bishopric came into our deacons quorum meeting. He asked if he could take a few minutes at the conclusion of the lesson. When the quorum adviser had finished, the member of the bishopric went to the blackboard, took a piece of chalk, and asked us to enumerate all the blessings for which we should be thankful at that Thanksgiving season. After he had listed twenty or thirty items he turned to the deacons quorum and said: "Brethren, I would hope that every deacon in this quorum would have a special prayer on Thanksgiving and that their family would kneel or bow in prayer and thank the Lord for all of these blessings. We really are blessed with much and we ought to be prayerful."

As he concluded his message a heavy cloud settled upon my heart. I wondered how we could ever have family prayer in my home. Conditions there were not like the normal Latter-day Saint home and I could not recall ever having had family prayer. I had always been fairly shy, and I did not know if I had enough courage to suggest it now. I thought about the bishopric's challenge throughout the remainder of the day and hoped that my older brother, who had also been at the meeting, would have the courage to ask Mother or Father if we could have a family prayer.

That evening at sacrament meeting our bishop said, "Brothers and Sisters, I hope there won't be one family in our ward who does not kneel on this Thanksgiving day and offer a special prayer of thanks to our Heavenly Father for all the blessings which each of us has received."

My heart began to weep. For the next three days I wondered how we could have prayer. On Wednesday night my father did not come home from work. Finally he staggered in in the middle of the night, inebriated, which caused great contention and argument in the home. As I heard this I thought: "How can we have prayer now. It looks like there is no possible way."

On Thanksgiving morning my brothers and sisters and I decided to go without breakfast so that we could eat as much Thanksgiving dinner as possible. To work up an appetite and pass the time until dinner, we went across the street to a vacant field and started digging a hole. We dug a hole six feet deep, six feet wide, and six feet across. Then we dug a trench about three feet deep, three feet wide, and about thirty-five feet long. With each shovel of dirt I thought: "How can we have family prayer? Is there a way? Will I have enough courage to say something at the right time?"

My mother called us to dinner just as we finished the hole. I hurried home, as hungry as I had ever been in my life. We all had ravenous appetites. After cleaning up we went and sat around the large oak table. Mother and Father still weren't speaking. I thought, "Now, will someone please suggest that we have a family prayer." But the suggestion did not come. Pretty soon Mother brought in the turkey, placed it on the table, and sat down. The food was passed and each plate was filled. I looked at my older brother with a heartfelt desire to communicate to him, to ask him to ask for family prayer. But he was unaware of what I was trying to communicate, and I didn't have the courage to ask. I sat there waiting and hoping that someone would say something. I tried to bring forth the words, but they wouldn't come. Finally everyone started eating. It was too late. The moment had passed.

Suddenly I was no longer hungry — not for food, at least. Instead my soul hungered as it had never hungered before to just say a prayer, a thankful prayer to a great and good Father in heaven who had watched over our family and blessed us with many of the blessings we had discussed in deacons quorum meeting the previous week.

I made a resolve at the dinner table that year that no son or daughter of mine would ever hunger for prayer as I did and not be able to have it, regardless of how quiet, shy or reserved that child might be. And I do not recall a day since I was married (other than when I was out of town) that my wife and I, and our children when they came, have not had prayer together.

That experience so many Thanksgivings ago gave me the resolve to make prayer a real and vital part of my life and the lives of my family. Make it a part of your life. Through prayer you will come to personally know your Father in heaven and his Son, Jesus Christ, and you will begin to develop that most important of all tools — spirituality.

Another valuable aid in developing spirituality is reading the scriptures. While we are frequently reminded of the importance of doing this, perhaps you avoid the scriptures, thinking that they are too difficult to read or that the message is too hard to understand. But if you will sincerely and honestly pray for an understanding of the scriptures, you will receive it.

Let me illustrate with a story about a young single woman who spent much of her spare time reading. She had a large library and had read nearly every book on the shelves. One night she decided to read a particular book which she had been deliberately avoiding for years. Reading it turned out to be an exhausting labor, but she kept with it until she finally finished the book. When she returned it to the bookshelf she made a mental note to herself, "That is the dullest book I have ever read."

A few days later she was invited to dinner with a gentleman friend. During dinner he asked her if she had ever read a particular book. She immediately recognized the title of the book she had just completed, and in her mind the mental note returned — "This is the dullest book I have ever read." But she did not express her opinion; she simply responded, "Yes, I've read the book."

In the ensuing weeks the two became well acquainted. One evening the subject of the book came up again. This time the young woman asked the gentleman's opinion of the book. "Highly favorable," he replied. "You see, I wrote it."

When he took her home that evening she went straight to the bookshelf, pulled out the book, and started reading it again. She read the last page just as the first streaks of dawn broke across the sky. As she closed the book and put it back on the shelf she made another mental note to herself: "This is the most beautiful book I have ever read."

The difference was that she knew the author.

The scriptures can become rich and meaningful to you as you come to know the Author. You will find that studying them can be one of the most thrilling and meaningful experiences of your life. I can personally testify that many choice spiritual experiences will come to you, as they have to me, in quiet, personal scripture study-time.

Trials and hardships can also be stepping stones toward spirituality if we will let them. The Lord never intended that life would be easy. Through the prophet Lehi he said, "It must needs be, that there is an opposition in all things." (2 Nephi 2:11.) But through opposition we can draw closer to our Heavenly Father.

One of the most beautiful stories of adversity that I have ever heard was told by Les Goates. I would like to include it so that you may better understand how hardships and trials increase your spirituality if you put them in their proper perspective.

" 'But as for me and my house,' began the welfare program in the old field west of Lehi on the Saratoga Road in the autumn of 1918. That was the terrible year of World War I during which more than fourteen million people died of that awful scourge, the black plague, or Spanish influenza.

"Winter came early that year and froze much of the sugar beet crop in the ground. My dad and my brother Francis were desperately trying each day to get one load of beets out of the frosty ground. They would plow the beets out of the ground, cut off the tops, toss the beets one at a time into the huge red beet wagon, then haul the load off to the sugar factory. It was slow and tedious work due to the frost and the lack of farm help. My brother Floyd and I were in the army, but Francis, or 'Franz' as everybody called him, was too young for military service.

"One evening while they were thus engaged in harvesting the family's only cash crop, a phone call came from our eldest brother, George Albert, superintendent of the State Industrial

School in Ogden. He bore the tragic news that Kenneth, nine-year-old son of our brother Charles (Charl), the school farm manager, had been stricken with the dreaded flu and after only a few hours of violent sickness had died on his father's lap. He asked if Dad would please come to Ogden and bring the boy home and lay him away in the family plot in the Lehi Cemetery.

"My father cranked up his old flap-curtained Chevrolet and headed for Five Points in Ogden to bring his little grandson home for burial. When he arrived at the home he found Charl sprawled across the cold form of Kenneth, the ugly brown discharge of the black plague oozing from his ears and nose and virtually burning up with fever.

" 'Take my boy home,' muttered the stricken young father, 'and lay him away in the family lot and come back for me tomorrow.'

"Father brought Kenneth home and made a coffin for him in his carpenter shop. Mother and our sisters, Jennie, Emma and Hazel, placed a cushion and a lining in it. Then Dad went with Franz and two kind neighbors to dig the grave. So many were dying that the families had to do the grave digging. A brief graveside service was all that was permitted.

"The folks had scarcely returned from the cemetery when the telephone rang again. George Albert (Bert) was on the line with another terrifying message: Charl had died, and two of Charl's beautiful little girls — Vesta, seven, and Elaine, five — were critically ill. Two of Bert's babies — Raeldon, four, and Pauline, three — had been stricken.

"Our good cousins, the Larkin Undertaking people, were able to obtain a casket for Charl and they sent him home in a railroad baggage car. Father and young Franz brought the body from the railroad station and placed it on the front porch of our old country home for an impromptu neighborhood viewing, but folks were afraid to come near the body of a black-plague victim. Father and Francis meanwhile had gone with neighbors to get the grave ready and arrange for a short service in which the great and noble spirit of Charles Hyrum Goates was commended into the keeping of his Maker.

"The next day my sturdy, unconquerable old dad was called on still another of his grim missions — this time to bring home Vesta, the smiling one with the raven hair and big blue eyes.

"When he arrived at the home he found Juliett, the grief-crazed mother, kneeling at the crib of darling little Elaine, the blue-eyed baby angel with the golden curls. Juliett was sobbing wearily and praying: 'Oh, Father in heaven, not this one, please! Let me keep my baby! Do not take any more of my darlings from me!'

"Before Father arrived home with Vesta the dread word had come again. Elaine had gone to join her daddy, brother Kenneth, and sister Vesta. And so it was that Father made another heartbreaking journey to bring home and lay away a fourth member of his family — all within the week.

"The telephone did not ring the evening of the day they laid away Elaine, nor were there any more sad tidings of death the next morning. It was assumed that George Albert and his courageous companion Della, although afflicted, had been able to save the little ones Raeldon and Pauline; and it was such a relief that cousin Reba Munns, a nurse, had been able to come in and help.

"After breakfast Dad said to Franz: 'Well, son, we had better get down to the field and see if we can get another load of beets out of the ground before they get frozen in any tighter. Hitch up and let's be on our way.'

"Francis drove the four-horse outfit down the driveway and Dad climbed aboard. As they drove along the Saratoga Road they passed wagon after wagon loaded with beets being hauled to the factory by neighborhood farmers. As they passed by, each driver would wave a greeting: 'Hi ya, Uncle George!' 'Sure sorry, George.' 'Tough break, George.' 'You've got a lot of friends, George.'

"On the last wagon rode the town comedian, the happy-go-lucky, redheaded, freckled-faced Jasper Rolfe. He waved a cheery greeting and called out, 'That's all of 'em, Uncle George.'

"My dad turned to Francis and said, 'I wish it was all of ours.'

"When they arrived at the farm gate, Francis jumped down off the big red beet wagon and opened the gate as Dad drove onto the field. He pulled up, stopped the team, paused a moment, and scanned the field from left to right and back and forth. Lo and behold, there wasn't a sugar beet on the whole field. Then it dawned upon Dad what Jasper Rolfe meant when he called out 'That's all of 'em, Uncle George!'

"Then Dad got down off the wagon and in his thumbless left hand picked up a handful of the rich, brown soil he loved so much and a beet top. He looked for a moment at these symbols of his labor, as if he couldn't believe his eyes.

"Then Father sat down on a pile of beet tops. This man who had brought four of his loved ones home for burial in the course of only six days, who had made caskets, dug graves, and even helped with the burial clothing, this amazing man who had never faltered, nor flinched, nor wavered throughout this agonizing ordeal, sat down on a pile of beet tops and sobbed like a little child.

"Then he arose, wiped his eyes with his big, red bandana handkerchief, looked up at the sky, and said, 'Thanks, Father.'"

This great man offered a prayer of gratitude to a kind and benevolent Father. Through adversity he had grown in spirituality. What a marvelous man! But this story has a double message. It also illustrates another important way of gaining spirituality — serving others.

I once had a young man ask me how to gain spirituality. At the time I was greeting Saints following the conclusion of a stake conference in Hawaii. A myriad of thoughts in answer to his question rushed through my mind. I thought, "If you had three or four hours we could discuss it and gain only a fragment of understanding." But as there was a long line of people waiting to shake hands, I simply asked, "Who is the most humble person you know?"

"I think the prophet is," he answered.

"I believe you are right," I responded. "What does he do more than almost any other man on the face of the earth?"

"I don't know," the man said.

"I think he serves — totally and without reservation," I replied. "I believe it is the degree of service we render to mankind that increases our humility and our spirituality." I believe he went away satisfied with that answer. As evidenced by the lives of our prophets, service will increase our spirituality.

We must also be willing to serve in any capacity to which we are called. I recall a story which President Lee told about a man who had been called by a member of the First Presidency to serve as a mission president. This man was an extremely successful business man with major business affairs. He told the member of the First Presidency that he would like to think over the calling before giving his answer. The man called a member of the Council of the Twelve and inquired as to what he thought he should do about the call to be a mission president. The apostle told him that he thought he didn't have any choice; he should willingly serve in any capacity the Lord desired. The man called a second apostle and received a similar response. Then he called a third and a fourth apostle; all of their answers were the same.

Finally the brother told the member of the First Presidency that he would accept the calling. The member of the First Presidency replied that they had already called someone else. "Perhaps you will be called again in the future," he said.

The man then went to President Harold B. Lee, then a member of the Quorum of the Twelve, and told him that the mission presidency call had been revoked. "My patriarchal blessing tells me that I will be a General Authority someday," the businessman said. "Do you think my delaying the answer to the call so long that it was revoked will have any effect upon my patriarchal blessing promise?" President Lee simply answered that he did not know.

Several months later President Lee sat in a Quorum of the Twelve meeting where names of men to serve as General Authorities were being suggested. President Lee later said that he turned pale as he heard this man's name considered and then passed over.

It doesn't matter where we are called to serve, but we ought to serve when we are called. And we ought to serve using all the talents with which the Lord has blessed us. To increase your spirituality, serve when called.

And lastly, to gain spirituality keep the commandments. There are many blessings to be gained from obedience to the commandments. Through keeping the law of tithing you may be financially rewarded. Obedience to the Word of Wisdom generally reaps a sound body and a healthy mind. Obeying the law of chastity results in inner tranquility and the companionship of the Spirit of the Lord. But the overriding benefit to be derived from obedience to any commandment is spirituality.

If you look at the most spiritual people you know, you will generally find that they have gained that spirituality through a lifetime of dedication to the teaching and commandments of the

Lord. Take President Spencer W. Kimball for an example, a stalwart in keeping the commandments from the time he was just a boy. Shortly after he was appointed to be an apostle in 1943, a man came to his office and related the following story:

"Spencer, your father was a prophet," the man began. "Your father made a prediction that has literally come to pass, and I want to tell you about it." He continued, "Your father talked with me at the corral one evening. I had brought a load of pumpkins for his pigs. You were just a little boy and you were sitting there milking the cows and singing to them as you milked. Your father turned to me and said: 'Brother, that boy, Spencer, is an exceptional boy. He always tries to mind me, whatever I ask him to do. I have dedicated him to be one of the mouthpieces of the Lord — the Lord willing. You will see him some day as a great leader. I have dedicated him to the service of God, and he will become a mighty man in the Church.' "

President Kimball related that story in his first general conference address after being called to the Quorum of the Twelve. Little did he know at that time that even greater spiritual challenges and rewards were to be his through his obedience to the commandments and through his devotion to the Lord.

When President Kimball was preparing to move from Arizona to Salt Lake City to fulfill his calling as an apostle, he came across his mother's patriarchal blessing. It was given to her when she was twenty-four years old and the mother of one child who had already passed away. None of her other ten children had yet been born. The patriarch had said: "Sister Olive Woolley, . . . thou shalt be numbered among the mothers in Israel and shall raise up a numerous posterity to the joy of thy husband. They shall grow up to become mighty men and women in the Church and Kingdom of God. Thy sons shall be stars of the first magnitude in thy crown and shall be healthy, strong, and vigorous in helping to direct the purposes of God in this last dispensation." While President Kimball had read this blessing many times in his life, he had never noticed before the line "Thy sons shall be stars of the first magnitude."

What a destiny was his! Yet, like you, his was always a do-it-yourself project. He was equipped with basically the same building tools which you have. He had every chance to succeed or fail that you have.

Each of us is the builder of his own soul and destiny. Each of us has on his hands the greatest do-it-yourself project of all time. The building rules are clear. The blueprint is established. And the tools are before you. What will you do with your block of wood? Remember, the King is expecting you to return to his presence. May you so live as to shape from your block of wood a life worthy to present before the King.

Index